Banishing Bureaucratese
Using Plain Language in Government Writing

D0627751

Banishing Bureaucratese

Using Plain Language in Government Writing

Judith Gillespie Myers

MANAGEMENTCONCEPTS

Vienna, Virginia

ſſſ
MANAGEMENTCONCEPTS

8230 Leesburg Pike, Suite 800
Vienna, Virginia 22182
Phone: (703) 790-9595
Fax: (703) 790-1371
Web: www.managementconcepts.com

Printed in the United States of America

Library of Congress Cataloging-in-Publication Data

Myers, Judith Gillespie, 1942–
    Banishing bureaucratese : using plain language in government
    writing / Judith Gillespie Myers.
        p. cm.
    Includes bibliographical references and index.
    ISBN 1-56726-101-9 (pbk.)
    1. Government report writing.   I. Title.

JF1525.R46 M94 2001
808'.066351—dc21

00-067898

To Geoff, Elizabeth, Randy, and Jennifer

About the Author

Judith Gillespie Myers, Ph.D., is an instructor and curriculum developer for Management Concepts, Inc., a training company in Vienna, Virginia. She has taught writing skills to hundreds of students, many of them government employees. She coauthored *Essentials of School Management* and has written more than 20 training manuals. As a journalist, radio newscaster, and news editor, Dr. Myers has written numerous articles and news items. She received her doctorate from American University in Washington, D.C.

Table of Contents

Preface

Effective writing skills are essential to business success. Whether you're writing a cover letter, a proposal, a technical report, or a simple email message, what and how you write affects how people interpret and respond to your message.

If you write on behalf of a government agency, your communication must be clear and understandable, especially when you are telling people how to obtain benefits or comply with requirements. Traditionally, government documents were written in legalistic, confusing language. Too often, this style resulted in reader frustration, lawsuits, and a lack of trust between citizens and their government.

This book is based on the guidelines for plain language issued by Vice President Gore in 1998, in response to a directive issued by President Clinton on June 1, 1998. The examples included in the book are taken from different agencies across the federal government, state and local governments, private documents, and sources outside the United States.

The purpose of this book is to provide specific, focused guidance for improving the use of language skills and writing methods. By learning the stages of writing and how to execute each stage, you can make writing easier and more enjoyable. This book is designed to help you:

- Write in reader-friendly, plain language

- Gain confidence in your ability to get the results you want when you write

- Recognize good writing and identify what makes it good

- Learn techniques that make writing better and easier to do

- Form good writing habits through structured practice, with immediate feedback

- Diagnose your writing skills to identify those needing improvement

- Formulate plans to continue your development.

These improved skills will help you become more effective in your business writing and in your personal writing as well.

When we use the term "business writing," we are referring to documents produced in the line of work, regardless of the specific workplace setting. Thus, memos, letters, and reports sent out by a government agency are as much business writing as those sent out by a corporation or a non-profit association. Although the guidelines presented in this book will help you with any kind of writing, including personal letters, the main focus of the book is on business, or workplace, writing.

Good writing skills are in demand by employers. The ability to write well correlates highly with the ability to think well—to analyze information, weigh alternatives, and make decisions. No one gets to the top without being able to write well.

Because writing is the process of getting thoughts onto paper, clear writing helps the writer develop, focus, and organize ideas. It helps writers understand their thoughts better.

Writing helps readers as well, because some information is too complex for oral communication alone. The written document aids both memory and understanding, and allows the reader to return to certain sections to review details.[1]

So organize your thoughts, write them clearly, present them effectively, and you're well on your way to success in the workplace.

Judith Gillespie Myers
Potomac, Maryland
December 2000

---

[1]Dumaine, Deborah. *Write to the Top: Writing for Corporate Success.* New York: Random House, 1989.

Acknowledgments

I would like to thank those who helped to make this book possible.

My thanks to Myra Strauss, for her careful editing; Jack Knowles, for his leadership and ideas; Beverly Copland, for her inspiration and persistence; Amy Carter, for her contributions; my sister, Anne Gillespie, for her enthusiasm and help; and my husband, Geoff, for his encouragement and patience.

I also am indebted to all of those who worked to develop the National Performance Review's Plain Language Network. Without their work, this book could not have been conceived. My gratitude goes especially to the former Plain Language Director Laurie Ford, for her time in reviewing the manuscript and her valuable suggestions.

PART I

Process and Stages of Plain Language Writing

CHAPTER I

Succeeding As a Writer in Today's Workplace

The Good, the Bad, and the Terrifying

Jane had been called into the office of Lee, her supervisor.

"Jane, we are going to give you a promotion. Congratulations!"

"Thank you," said Jane, hardly able to contain her surprise.

"There's one thing you need to know about this promotion," said Lee. "It entails much more writing. You will be expected to send out detailed letters, as well as frequent memos and occasional reports. Eventually, you may be asked to edit some work done by staff."

Jane had mixed feelings about her promotion. On the one hand, she was happy about the increase in salary and in responsibility. On the other hand, she was worried about the prospect of writing. Jane did not have much experience writing, frequently experienced "writer's block," and found the entire process terrifying.

"I guess I'd better brush up on my business writing skill," Jane said to herself.

To succeed in the workplace, whether you are in government or elsewhere, you must be able to express yourself effectively, clearly, and persuasively. You must create documents that your readers will read and understand, documents that result in decisions, documents that affect your readers as you intend. Each letter, report, or email that you send out is a reflection on your organization. And it is a reflection on you.

Like Jane, you may find the whole process of writing daunting. Many of us do. And yet, with the right guidance and practice, we can all become better and more effective writers.

COMMON MYTHS ABOUT BUSINESS WRITING

One reason that many people dread writing is because certain myths have become associated with business writing and with the writing process. Do these sound familiar?

1. *Myth: The first rule of business writing is to be business-like, so a business letter has to sound somewhat unnatural.*

   Reality: Business letters should sound natural, but professional. While the tone of your letter depends on the context, purpose, and audience, you want to sound friendly and sometimes even informal. The increased use of email has led to more informality in correspondence, so today's letters are typically more conversational than those in the past.

2. *Myth: To convey technical or legal information, your document must sound intellectual and sophisticated.*

   Reality: Your primary goal in conveying technical or legal information is to make sure the reader understands what you're writing. To achieve this goal, you need to write simply and directly. Joseph Kimble refutes the notion that plain language will "dumb down" important government communication:

   > As for the notion that plain language is unsophisticated, once again just the reverse is true. It is much harder to simplify than to complicate. Anybody can take the sludge from formbooks, thicken it with a few more provisions, and leave it at that. Only the best minds and best writers

can cut through. In short, writing simply and directly only *looks* easy. It takes skill and work and fair time to compose—all part of the lawyer's craft.[1]

The same is true of technical information: It must be clear and straightforward so that anyone can understand it, regardless of his or her technical background. In fact, focus group results show that even technical experts do not always understand technical language easily or quickly.

3. *Myth: In business writing, it is important to impress your readers with your mastery of the subject.*

    Reality: While this was the goal of college writing, the purpose of business writing is to:

    - Inform

    - Persuade

    - Explain or clarify

    - Propose ideas

    - Solve problems

    - Instruct.

    While students tend to use complex sentences and long words to demonstrate their knowledge of a subject, business writers need to use short sentences and words and to concentrate on delivering a clear, understandable message.

4. *Myth: Really good writers write it right the first time, without revising their drafts.*

Reality: Very few people can write a polished paragraph on the first try. Good writing involves many rewrites and may include complete reorganization. Even after an experienced writer has worked on a manuscript, it goes to a professional editor for revision and polishing before being published.

F. Scott Fitzgerald revised his stories at least five times before they were published.

Ernest Hemingway told a reporter once that he wrote the ending to *A Farewell to Arms* 39 times before he was satisfied. When asked what it was that stumped him, Hemingway responded, "Getting the words right."

5. *Myth: Grammar and punctuation are the most important points in learning to write well.*

Reality: The most important point is to communicate your message clearly. If the reader doesn't understand what you're saying, why bother to write? However, having an error in grammar or punctuation is like walking out of the house in your best formal attire with a catsup stain on your shirt: It detracts from the message.

6. *Myth: You need to keep control of your writing. This means correcting each idea as it comes to you, before you put it down on paper.*

Reality: As soon as your ideas start flowing, you should begin writing so you won't lose them; you can always go back later and make minor modifications. As we will discuss later, it is important to divide writing into stages and not to mix the stages of writing. In the stage of drafting, you want to capture those first thoughts— not censor them.

Natalie Goldberg describes first thoughts this way:

> First thoughts have tremendous energy. It is the way the mind first flashes on something. The internal censor usually squelches them, so we live in the realm of second and third thoughts, thoughts on thought, twice and three times removed from the direct connection of the first fresh flash . . . First thoughts are also unencumbered by ego, by that mechanism in us that tries to be in control. . . .[2]

7. *Myth: You should strive for long sentences and long words in business documents.*

Reality: A document with long sentences and many syllables is considered more difficult to read than one with shorter sentences and fewer syllables. For most business writing, the ideal sentence length is 15 to 20 words, or about an 8th or 9th grade reading level.

The writers of *Using Reader-Friendly Documents* (developed by the National Partnership for Reinventing Government) point out the importance of short sentences:

> The best way to tell your reader what you want is a short, straightforward sentence. Complex sentences overloaded with dependent clauses and exceptions confuse the reader by losing the main point in a forest of words. Resist the temptation of put everything in one sentence; break up your idea into its various parts and make each one the subject of its own sentence.[3]

8. *Myth: A document is a document. Once you learn how to write, you can use the same design and style from one workplace to the next.*

Reality: You need to consider your organization's *culture.* Consider, for example, the difference between an office in the U.S. Department of Defense that deals with top-secret information and an office in a county recreation department that staffs local parks. The recreation department probably would have a much more informal environment, and that informality would be reflected in its documents.

The style of documents you write depends on the mission of your organization as well as the mission of your specific office. A letter from the Office of the Under Secretary of Defense for Personnel and Readiness to a prospective employee would differ dramatically from a letter from the Office of the Assistant to the Secretary of Defense for Intelligence Oversight describing lapses in intelligence in an Army installation. Noting the conventions, practices, and mission of your organization will help you compose appropriate, professional documents.

9. *Myth: Workplace communication can be handled easily with boilerplate forms.*

   Reality: While most offices have form letters that they use for routine correspondence, serious communication rarely fits into such a form. Such issues require careful consideration of purpose, audience, context, and message.

10. *Myth: Administrative assistants handle nearly all writing responsibilities.*

    Reality: In today's environment, most workers have to compose their own correspondence, reports, and, of course, email. Even high-level managers who have assistants to write routine correspondence must approve such documents. And they must compose letters or reports for any non-routine or complex situations. With the proliferation of computers and downsizing, more managers are taking responsibility for their own correspondence rather than dictating to an assistant.

THE IMPORTANCE OF PLAIN LANGUAGE IN GOVERNMENT WRITING

You can reduce confusion or misinterpretation in all your writing while still giving readers the technical information they need. The best way to do this is to:

- Engage your readers

- Write clearly

- Put the main idea first

- Write in a visually appealing style.

Government writing presents a special challenge. Government documents often contain technical information, and they go out to multiple audiences—some highly knowledgeable, some less so.

Government documents have traditionally contained "gobbledygook"—jargon and complicated, legalistic language. These uninviting letters and reports sound like they are addressed to technical experts and lawyers rather than to readers who need to be influenced or informed.

Presidential Efforts to Improve Government Writing

For decades, presidents have urged clear writing in government documents. For example, Franklin Roosevelt despaired over the following blackout order during World War II:

> Such preparations shall be made as will completely obscure all Federal buildings and non-Federal buildings occupied by the government during an air raid for any period of time from visibility by reason of internal or external illumination.

"Tell them," Roosevelt said, "that in buildings where they have to keep the work going to put something across the windows."[4]

However, federal documents continued to be filled with "bureaucratese." In an attempt to cut the government gobbledygook, President Carter signed an executive order directing that federal regulations be written "simply and clearly." Other presidents have made similar efforts.

The most recent program to improve government writing was President Clinton's 1998 directive requiring agencies to use plain English. Vice President Gore issued guidance on how to implement this memo. Then several agencies set up the Plain Language Action Network (PLAN), a government-wide group that works to improve communications from the federal government to the public. Each agency has a plain language official, and the government awards those agencies that make significant improvements in their documents. The PLAN Web site (www.plainlanguage.gov) contains numerous resources to help writers communicate more clearly.

The following is taken from President Clinton's Memorandum of June 1, 1998:

> The Federal Government's writing must be in plain language. By using plain language, we send a clear message about what the Government is doing, what it requires, and what services it offers. Plain language saves the Government and the private sector time, effort, and money.
>
> Plain language requirements vary from one document to another, depending on the intended audience. Plain language documents have logical organization, easy-to-read design features, and use:
>
> - common, everyday words, except for necessary technical terms;
> - "you" and other pronouns;
> - the active voice; and
> - short sentences.[5]

Plain Language in Legal Documents

Although "legalese" was historically the accepted style for statutes and regulations, more organizations are encouraging plain language:

- Many states have laws requiring that consumer statutes be written in plain language. The Federal Judicial Center in Washington teaches federal judges to write their opinions in plain English.[6]

- The U.S. Securities and Exchange Commission has drafted a *Plain English Handbook*.

- The American Bar Association has issued the following resolution encouraging agencies to write regulations in plain language:

  > **RESOLVED,** That the American Bar Association urges agencies to use plain language in writing regulations, as a means of promoting the understanding of legal obligations, using such techniques as:
  >
  > - Organizing them for the convenience of their readers;
  > - Using direct and easily understood language;
  > - Writing in short sentences, in the active voice; and
  > - Using helpful stylistic devices, such as question-and-answer formats, vertical lists, spacing that facilitates clarity, and tables.
  >
  > To avoid problems in the use of plain language techniques, agencies should:
  >
  > - Take into account possible judicial interpretations as well as user understanding;
  > - Clearly state the obligations and rights of persons affected, as well as those of the agency; and
  > - Identify and explain all intended changes when revising regulations.

- The Department of Interior has revised all of its regulations to comply with plain language standards. Some good examples are the Bureau of Indian Affairs' Housing Improvement Program and the Mineral Management Service's rules on relief or reduction of royalty rates.

- The Bureau of Land Management (BLM) writes all rules in plain language. One recent example is a regulation regarding mining on public lands—one of Interior Secretary Babbitt's highest priorities.

- The National Labor Relations Board (NLRB) has issued a revised edition of its style manual, first published in 1983. *The NLRB Style Manual: A Guide for Legal Writing in Plain English* gives guidelines for writing briefs and other documents submitted to the Board and to the Division of Judges.

- The Canadian Bar Association and the Canadian Bankers Association established a Joint Committee on Plain Language Documentation in 1988.[7]

- Even the *Federal Register* is considering changing its look. A new proposed format will make it easier to read. It contains the following changes:

  —The preamble summary has bullets.

  —A half-line is inserted between paragraphs.

  —The first line of sections and subsections is indented.

  —Vertical lines instead of horizontal lines are used in tables.

  —The document has two columns instead of three.[8]

In Chapter 12, we give guidelines on writing regulations. You will also see some examples of "before" and "after" versions of regulations that were rewritten in plain language.

CHANGES AFFECTING WORKPLACE COMMUNICATION

Regardless of your workplace, four changes have affected workplace communication, according to Jo Allen—increasing technology, workplace diversity, globalization, and collaboration.[9]

Technology

Twenty-five years ago, the American workplace looked very different from what it is today. Secretaries sat at front desks typing formal letters for their bosses. Sometimes they would be interrupted by a phone call, a visitor, or a request from the boss to take dictation.

Managers sat at desks cluttered with papers and perhaps stacks of books for gleaning information. They frequently attended meetings or visited with employees in field offices. If there was not time for a meeting, managers sent paper memos to those in other offices.

Any employees who needed training had to arrange to be away from their offices and to find other employees to cover the phones.

Today, secretaries have been replaced by administrative assistants, many of whom work for three or four bosses. They produce letters on computers and frequently fax or even email memos, letters, or reports to internal or external customers.

Managers work at computers and conduct research on the Internet. They have instant communication by email to colleagues, staff, or customers, and they stay in touch with "virtual teams" through teleconferences.

Employees who want training frequently can find what they need on the Internet or on a compact disc. Even if they opt for classroom instruction instead of distance learning, they do not need to be concerned about covering the phones, since voice mail can take their messages.

Technological change has dramatically affected workplace communication. Most of these changes are positive, though some are negative.

Because of the increased use of email, written communication—especially within an organization—is much more informal. People are much more likely to ignore traditional formatting and grammatical rules. Because information is generated and transferred so much more rapidly, workers can find data they need within minutes. Therefore, reports can be created and disseminated much more rapidly.

More sophisticated technology makes increased demands on employees, however. Employees must be able to navigate the Internet, sift through large volumes of information, and glean the data needed. Government agencies create and maintain Web sites, which must be kept current and accurate.

In addition, information overload plagues workers more than ever before. Employees at all levels are spending increasing amounts of time reading and responding to email, listening to voice mail, and sifting through Internet documents.

With the increased number of computers in the workplace, workers in a wide range of positions are expected to have written communication skills. Even employees in most types of technical positions are expected to write coherent memos and to generate clear, understandable letters and reports.

Workplace Diversity

The past few decades have seen an increased commitment to hiring and promoting minorities and women. The government has led the way in promoting workplace diversity and has become more diverse itself. As a result, men and women of various ages and ethnic backgrounds are working side by side in work groups or on special projects. This workplace diversity has brought a richness of talent, outlook, and communication style. However, it requires skill in both oral and written communication, as well as an awareness of attitudes and expectations—both one's own and others'. It requires attention to the connotations of messages and care to avoid misunderstanding.

For example, a person writing an email to a colleague for whom English is a second language would need to avoid English idioms that might be misunderstood, such as "just dropping by," "drawing the line," or "beating around the bush." Also, men and women need to exercise care and professionalism in workplace relations. The joking and sexual innuendoes once tolerated on the job are no longer acceptable and can even lead to legal charges of sexual harassment. Every effort must be made to accommodate workers with disabilities and to help them become comfortable and productive in the workplace.

Globalization

Organizations in both the private and public sectors are dealing more and more with individuals and groups from many nations.

The influence of globalization can be seen in a variety of venues. Americans are finding that they must change some of their familiar habits or ways of doing business so that they don't offend business associates from other countries.

For example:

- In Japan and the Pacific Rim, personal relationships and friendships are very important. It may take longer than most Americans are accustomed to taking to establish business relationships.

- In Europe, peoples' titles carry more weight than in America.

- Business agreements in the Middle East do not always have the same permanence as they do in America.

The old saying, "The medium is the message" is especially true in international relations. It's a good idea to find out which medium is the most common and acceptable for a given international organization—email, letter, fax, telephone, or face-to-face meeting. Any form of communication with individuals of other nationalities often must be clearer and more formal than communication with fellow Americans.

Collaboration

Organizations of all sizes and types are discovering the benefits of collaboration and teamwork. Teams meet to brainstorm about projects and bring varying perspectives to the problem-solving process. This collaboration increases both morale and the quality of a product or service.

Teams often work together on writing projects. They plan together and define the audience, purpose, and content of the document as well as its organization. Team members may each write a part of the document, then edit each other's work. Or, one team member may do research while another team member drafts the document and a third team member edits the work. Then they work together on the final design of the document.

In today's workplace, each document is read by at least one other person—often several. The days of writing papers that come back with few marks except a compliment to the writer are gone. Standards are different, but, on the positive side, they are more realistic. No one is expected to know everything, get it all right the first time, or write an error-free paper.

The workplace thus values different skills and attributes than academia does. To be successful in their jobs, writers must be able to work in teams and to take constructive criticism. This demands:

- Different attitudes, skills, and perspectives

- The ability to assess the strengths and weaknesses of teammates

- Knowledge about how groups work and the stages they go through

- Expertise in dividing work, making assignments, and scheduling and tracking large projects.

TEST YOURSELF: SELF-ASSESSMENT

The following statements express feelings that many people have about their writing problems. Do you share these feelings? How strongly? For each statement, indicate:

1 always or almost always

2 frequently

3 sometimes

4 seldom

5 very rarely or never

In the column on the right, you will find the section of this book that deals with each of these issues.

Score	Statement	Chapter(s)
	I have trouble getting started.	Chapter 2
	I have trouble organizing my ideas.	Chapter 2
	I probably say too much.	Chapters 3 and 5
	I probably say too little.	Chapter 5
	People have to follow up to ask me, "What did you mean by that?"	Chapter 5
	My writing sounds forced, unnatural, not like me.	Chapter 4
	I'm unsure about how formal or businesslike I should be.	Chapter 4
	I doubt that what I write is grammatically correct.	Chapter 7
	My attempts to revise my writing don't seem to improve it much.	Chapter 7
	I spend too much time writing for the results I get.	Chapters 2 and 3
	My documents do not seem to look visually appealing.	Chapter 6
	I'm uncomfortable sending email, because I don't know how to express myself well.	Chapter 8
	I don't know how to organize a letter—or how to get started.	Chapter 9
	Report writing is difficult for me.	Chapter 10

Score	Statement	Chapter(s)
	People do not seem to understand my technical writing.	Chapter 11
	I don't know how to prepare an effective presentation.	Chapter 12
	When working on a group writing project, I'm never certain about my responsibilities.	Chapter 12

If you face workplace-writing tasks with dread and fear, you're not alone. Many people share these feelings. Because of common misconceptions, many of us take the wrong approach to writing. We need to learn how to divide the writing process into stages, adapt our writing to fit the workplace, and produce more reader-friendly documents.

The government setting presents some unique challenges to writers because of both the audience and the type of information being conveyed. In an effort to improve public-sector writing, the Clinton Administration issued the Plain Language directive. Guidelines from this directive are given throughout this book.

Regardless of the workplace setting, four trends have affected business writing: technology, diversity, globalization, and collaboration. Being aware of these changes—and making the most of them—can enhance your writing experience and improve your documents.

---

[1]Kimble, Joseph. "Answering the Critics of Plain Language." *The Scribes Journal of Legal Writing (1994-1995)*. <plainlanguage.gov/library/kimble.htm>

[2]Goldberg, Natalie. *Writing Down the Bones: Freeing the Writer Within*. Boston: Shambhala, 1986, p. 9.

[3]*Using Writer-Friendly Documents*. <www.plainlanguage.gov>

[4]Cited in Zinsser, William. *On Writing Well*. Second ed. New York: Harper & Row, 1980, p. 8.

[5]<plainlanguage.gov/cites/memo.htm>

[6]Wilson, Carol Ann. "Be on the Cutting Edge: Learn These Seven Plain Language Principles Now!" <www.wwlia.org/plainlan.htm>

[7]Ibid.

[8]See <www.nara.gov/fedreg/plainlan.html> for more information on the redesign of the *Federal Register* format.

[9]Allen, Jo. *Writing in the Workplace*. Boston: Allyn and Bacon, 1998, pp. 18-22. Adapted by permission.

CHAPTER 2

Getting Started:
The Planning Stage

Battling Writer's Block

In the middle of an extremely busy week, Tom was asked to provide a letter of recommendation for a former employee, Marcia, for admission to engineering school.

Tom sat at his computer and stared at the screen. No ideas came to mind. His mind wandered, and he thought about the things he had to accomplish before the weekend. He was distracted by a conversation outside in the hall. He stared again at the screen and gritted his teeth. Then he remembered what he needed to do: gather information and prepare an outline.

Before planning the letter, Tom collected the data he needed. He re-read the instructions from the engineering school to determine exactly what he needed to do. He located a copy of Marcia's resume and a brief biography that appeared in the agency newsletter. Then he talked to some people who had worked with Marcia so that he could find out more about her specific knowledge, skills, and abilities, her work habits, and her ways of interacting with co-workers. Finally, he called Marcia and asked her about her purpose for attending engineering school and her plans for the future. He asked Marcia to fax him her personal statement written for her application.

Tom then went to lunch and spent the hour thinking about what he wanted to say in the letter. He reflected on Marcia's outstanding qualities. Then he thought about what an engineering school admission officer would want to know.

After Tom returned to his desk, he made the following informal outline:

Recommendation for Marcia Thompson

- How I know Marcia
  —worked with her for three years
  —collaborated on many projects
  —specific project: inspection of bridges
- Personal observations of Marcia's competence handling the XYZ Project
- Hallmark of her character: honesty
- Observations by teammates of Marcia's interpersonal skills and work habits
- Marcia's thoroughness and adherence to quality
- Comments from customers regarding Marcia's abilities and responsiveness
- Reasons why Marcia could benefit from engineering school
- What Marcia could contribute to engineering school

All of us have felt the way Tom did as he faced his writing task. Whether writing a long report or a memo, we find ourselves staring at the blank screen, our minds wandering. At those times, the writing process can seem so overwhelming that we'd do anything to avoid putting down that first word.

If you are having a difficult time getting started and think you may be experiencing writer's block, try the following:

- *Avoid leaving your project until the last minute.* You'll need time to prepare, plan, write, get away from your project, and edit it.

- *When scheduling your project, give yourself some time to warm up to the topic.* Let your mind wander. Many of your best ideas will occur to you at odd moments during the day or night. But try to set a time limit for this step.

- *Jot down every idea that comes to you, quickly and randomly.* If you find it easier, discuss your project with a colleague or talk into a tape recorder. You can dictate much faster—some say six times faster—than you can write.

- *If you run into a roadblock after you get started, take a break and let your ideas "cook" or incubate.* When you return in a few minutes or hours, you can select the essential ideas, add new ideas, and delete irrelevant ideas.

- *Don't confuse writing with editing.* Writing can proceed much more easily if writers understand the phases in the writing process. These phases or steps are:

  —Planning

  —Drafting

  —Editing.

Although you may move back and forth from one stage to another, the important thing to remember is not to combine the stages. Each stage requires a distinctly different process and way of thinking. For example, during the drafting phase, you should not be editing. Drafting requires that you allow your thoughts to flow freely. If you try to edit while you draft, you will inhibit the flow of ideas.

GUIDELINES FOR PLANNING

It pays to take the time to plan ahead before you begin writing—even when your message is short and even when you have to write under deadline pressure. It's like looking at a road map before you start driving to a new destination: If you know where you're going before you start, you're less likely to get lost along the way.

For any kind of writing—email, letter, or report—you need to make sure that you understand three things: (1) your purpose; (2) your audience; and (3) your subject.

Know Your Purpose

Before you begin, ask yourself why you are writing.

If you are carrying out an assigned writing project, get as much guidance as possible before beginning.

If this is *not* an assigned writing project, ask yourself the following questions before you start:

- Should *I* be writing this? At this time?

- Would a phone call or meeting be more effective?

- Am I too late to send this?

- Is someone else communicating the same information? Should I check with that person?

- Should I include deadlines? What actions, if any, should I request?

- How should I send this?

    —E-mail

    —Traditional mail

    —Fax.

Decide what effect you want to have on your reader. Identify the most important idea—the one you want the reader to remember. A one- or two-sentence purpose statement helps get you started. It forces you to decide exactly *why* you are writing. It directs your effort and becomes the lens through which you view the entire writing project. Your purpose statement becomes the lead-in to your outline and then often becomes the first words in the document itself.

When writing your purpose statement, ask yourself:

- What's the best outcome for my agency? What do I need to say to get this outcome?

- What's the best outcome for the reader? What do I need to say to get this outcome?

Know Your Audience

In *Using Writer-Friendly Documents,* the writers give the following advice:

> Identify your audience early and think about why the reader needs to read the document. Identify people who will be interested, even if they are not directly affected. Write to everyone who is interested, not just to technical or legal experts. Keep in mind the average reader's level of technical expertise.[1]

To determine your reader's technical expertise, you need to consider his or her *role*. For example, a network engineer has different responsibilities, and a different type of expertise, than a personnel manager. Typically, the role of your reader determines what the reader knows about your subject, the reader's *decision-making level*, and the type or form of information needed.

Your reader's technical expertise will in turn tell you what kind of background information you must supply to guide your readers from Point A to Point B in as straight a line as possible. Also, your reader's knowledge of your subject will determine what kind of technical jargon and acronyms would be appropriate, or inappropriate.

The chart on the facing page illustrates the categories of readers, their decision-making levels, their knowledge of the subject, and the type or form of information they need. Although this chart applies to readers of *technical information,* it is also a useful guide for other types of information.

Regardless of the role of your reader, you need to determine how he or she will react to your document. Are you delivering good news or bad news? Will the reader like your recommendations or resist them? Should you state your case forcefully, or will that make the reader defensive? To gauge your reader's reaction, Sheryl Lindsell-Roberts recommends that you ask yourself the following questions:

- Are your disputing the data?

- Will your reader lose face by accepting your recommendations?

- Will your message create more work for your reader?

- Will your reader get pressure from his manager because of your message?[2]

Once you have answered these questions, you can write your document in a way that minimizes negative reactions.

A document often has many readers. You may be writing to exporters and importers, or coal miners and surface owners, or airlines and passengers. Even if your document goes to only one person, others may read it later. When you write to multiple readers who have a similar knowledge of, and attitude toward, your subject, you can write to one representative person in the audience.

Categories of Readers

Categories of Readers	Managers	Experts or advisors (engineers, accountants)	Operators (field technicians, office workers, salespersons)	General readers ("laypersons")
Decision-Making Level	High level. Will translate your document into action.	Medium level. Analyze information and may influence decision-makers.	Low level. Receive information and adjust jobs accordingly.	Typically low.
Knowledge of Subject	Typically have general understanding but are removed from hands-on detail.	Understand technical aspects of the subject that apply to them.	Understand technical aspects of subject that apply to them.	Usually have least amount of information on the topic.
Type/Form of Information Needed	Brief summaries, background information—the big picture.	Technical details, tables and charts, and appendices of supporting information.	Clear organization, well-written instructions, clarity about how document affects their job	Definitions of technical terms, frequent graphs, clear statements about how the document affects them.

But what if your intended readers have different levels of knowledge or interest or different roles? What do you do? The following are guidelines for writing regulations and letters for diverse audiences.

Writing Regulations

In *Using Reader-Friendly Documents*, the authors recommend that you do the following when writing to diverse audiences:

- Break your document down into essential elements.

- Determine which elements apply to each part of your audience.

- Group the elements according to who is affected. If you are writing about research grants, first tell the professors what they have to do, and then tell the university accounting department what it has to do.

- Clearly identify to whom you are speaking in each section. Don't make a reader go through material only to find out at the end that the section doesn't apply.[3]

Writing Letters and Reports

When you are writing a letter, you generally write to only one person. However, you must consider any additional readers. For example, if you write to a member of Congress about a constituent problem, someone in the Congress member's office may attach a cover letter and send it on to the constituent without any further explanation. Therefore, you must write so that both audiences understand your letter.

Distinguish between primary readers (such as the member of Congress) and secondary readers (such as the constituent). *Primary readers* are those who have the greatest need to know. They are the decision-makers, the ones who will need to act after reading your report. Therefore, they are the ones you should cater to. *Secondary readers* are those who, while interested, do not need the same level of detail.

For reports, Maryann Piotrowski recommends that you consider including the following for both sets of readers:

1. A cover memo providing background information and guidance

2. An executive summary of your report

3. Headings

4. Marginal notations

5. A table of contents for anyone who needs the "nitty-gritty"

6. Appendices for information of interest only to specialists.[4]

Know Your Subject

Once you've determined your purpose and identified your audience, you need to research your subject. Collect all the information you need (but don't overdo it).

- Review:

  —Correspondence

  —Policy directives

—Administrative memorandums, or any other papers related to your task.

- Consult with people who can lend knowledge or insight.

- Analyze your notes or your data collection.

- Digest the material.

- Sift through it to determine what is useful and what is not.

- Organize useful material into meaningful groups.

GUIDELINES FOR ORGANIZING AND OUTLINING

Once you have determined your purpose, audience, and subject, think about what you have to say. The larger your writing project, the more you need to plan and prepare a useful outline.

Why write an outline?

- The outline provides structure and organization.

- It shows you visibly if you have enough information. For example, if your outline includes only one subheading for a topic, you know that you need to either get more data or delete the topic.

- It speeds up the review process when someone in the organization must approve the document. It is much easier to make changes at the outline stage, before you invest time in the draft. And reviewers who approve an outline are much less likely to request major changes later.[5]

Outlines can take several different forms.

The Traditional Outline

This is the standard (or *Harvard*) outline, with its formal framework of Roman and Arabic numerals and upper- and lower-case letters, arranged with indentations and headings of equal importance. An example might be:

Proposal to Relocate
I. Overview
II. Reasons to consider relocating
   A. Increased business
      1. New contract with XYZ Corporation
      2. Negotiating contract with ABC Corporation
         a. Negotiations almost concluded
         b. Need to assure ABC that we can fulfill contract terms
   B. Decreased costs

The traditional outline can be written either by hand or on the computer, using the outline view in Word. The advantage of using a computer in the outlining stage is that it allows you to see your ideas as they occur and to reorganize those ideas easily.

The Question-Based Outline

Create an imaginary dialogue in which you play two parts: the writer and the reader. List questions *the reader will ask*, and write your answers underneath. Answer your questions as clearly and completely as possible. Then organize those ideas into a traditional outline.

The following are some examples:

Making a presentation:

1. What is this about?
2. Why should I pay attention to it?
3. What's the objective?
4. How will the objective be achieved?
5. How much will it cost?
6. How long will it take?
7. What are the risks?
8. What's the potential payoff?
9. What's the next step?

Conveying information:

1. What's this about?
2. What does it mean to me?
3. What are the details?
4. Which parts are most important?
5. What am I supposed to do about it?
6. How do I start?

Making an interim report:

1. What's this about?
2. Is the project on track?
3. What problems is the writing encountering?
4. Anything for me to worry about?
5. Any action required of me?

The Brainstorm Outline

A brainstorm outline (also called mind mapping) uses a nonlinear, pictorial way of presenting ideas and their relationship to each other. To brainstorm:

- In the center of a large piece of paper, write your main idea for the project (for example, "proposal for new software").

- Draw lines radiating outward from that main purpose. Each line represents a main idea you want to present (for example, "costs").

- Along each line, draw smaller lines representing related or supporting ideas (for example, "software").

- Continue this process, throwing in ideas as they occur to you, until you have developed a wheel-like picture (as shown below) of the ideas you want to cover.

- Organize those ideas into a traditional outline.

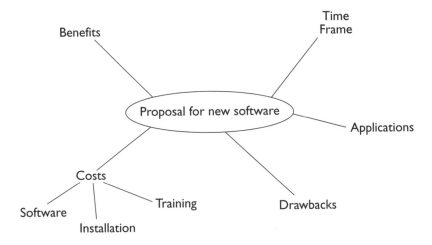

Index Cards

This tried-and-true term paper technique allows you to rearrange ideas easily. Simply use one card for each item of information you want to cover, and then sort the cards, arranging them into piles of similar topics.

Sticky Notes or Movable Tape

Like index cards, these allow you to rearrange your ideas easily. Simply write down one idea on each note or strip of tape, and then arrange them on a large piece of paper.

Checklist

Use this system to generate and arrange your ideas. The checklist would include a list of words and phrases that cover key points, with space to insert examples, facts, and other supporting material as you go along.

Semiformal Outline

This is a compromise between the standard outline and the checklist system. In this outline, you can show major ideas and the levels of ideas subordinate to them. You may choose to use capitalization, dashes, numbers, indentations, or other means to show the relationships between ideas.

Free Writing

If you cannot come up with any ideas using the above methods, try simply writing down whatever comes to mind:

I really can't think of what to say about this topic. I wonder what I should do for lunch. Maybe if we move, we could find a building with a deli nearby. That would be nice, because our clients could use it, too. That would make our clients happy, and maybe help with our word-of-mouth. There goes Steve. I wonder if he's heard about the ABC negotiations. If we get that, we would need more space for production. . . .

As you can see, the writer has already generated two ideas about why the organization should consider moving (". . . help with our word-of-mouth . . ." and ". . . more space for production. . . ."). Later, the writer can review the text and use an outline to organize ideas.

Whatever system you use to generate and organize your ideas, don't hesitate to revise and reorganize the outline as the writing proceeds.

Techniques for Organizing and Generating Ideas	Try . . .
When you . . .	
don't know where to start	free writing or question asking
need to organize and convey a large amount of information and overlook nothing	brainstorming or listing ideas
are taking notes in the field, interviewing a lot of people	using Post-Its or a tape recorder
know exactly what you want to say and have a clear plan in mind	a formal outline
have a document that requires extensive research	index cards

What are the steps in going from informal techniques (index cards, Post-Its, free writing, or a checklist) to writing a traditional outline?

1. Record random ideas quickly into a "nonlinear" (messy) outline. Use free association to scribble down points.

2. Show relationships. Survey your page of ideas, locate the three or four main points that indicate the direction your document will take, and circle them. Then draw lines to connect these main points to their supporting points.

3. Arrange the points in an order that makes sense.

4. Draft a final outline. Whether you use a Harvard (traditional format with Roman numerals, etc.) outline or a more informal style, you should include the following features:

   — Depth. Be sure the entire outline has enough support to develop the draft.

   — Balance. Include enough detail for all your main points. Make sure that each part has at least two subdivisions.

   — Parallel form. Give points in the same grouping the same grammatical form. For example, you should use either topics or complete sentences for all your points.

GUIDELINES FOR SEQUENCING YOUR IDEAS

After you have generated ideas and produced some kind of an outline, check over your outline to make sure that you have put your ideas in the best order for impact. When you use the appropriate method of development, your readers are drawn to your ideas and can follow your line of thought. Below are the most common ways to sequence your ideas, depending on whether the goal is to inform or to persuade.

Documents to Inform

- *Inverted pyramid.* Memo announcing a meeting. Give the most important information first.

- *Order of familiarity.* Explanation of how a new system or product operates. Go from the most familiar to the least.

- *Order of location* (spatial or geographic order). Description of new office building.

- *Alphabetical order.* Biographies of new employees.

- *Chronological order.* Annual reports, minutes of meetings, case histories.

- *Category order.* Deals with topics that go together. Classifies ideas into reasonable categories.

- *Inductive order* (going from specific examples to generalized conclusions). Articles for trade publications.

- *List.* Memo to boss giving projects you're working on.

- *Order for comparison.* Two or more ideas, products, places, or employees. You have two choices: (1) point-by-point comparison, or (2) block comparison.

- *Deductive order.* Memo explaining a new idea, e.g., why you need new computer software. Start with the general principle and support it with examples.

Documents to Persuade

- *Statement of reasons method.* This method is very similar to the category order method for documents to inform, except that each main point is a reason why your readers should accept and agree with your point of view.

- *Comparative advantages method.* As you look at a list of reasons why your readers should accept your point of view, you may see that the best reasons may be phrased as advantages over the procedure now in practice.

- *Problem-solution method.* The main points should be formulated to show that:

    —there is a problem that requires a change in attitude or behavior;

    —the solution you are presenting will solve the problem; and

    —your solution is the best possible solution to this particular problem.

- *Most acceptable to least acceptable.* Useful when you know or can predict what the reader is likely to accept or reject.

TEST YOURSELF: SELECTING THE PURPOSE AND SEQUENCE

Read the following paragraphs. Select the paragraph that states the purpose. Put a "1" next to it. Then use the numbers 2, 3, 4, and 5 to indicate the appropriate sequence for the remaining paragraphs of the letter.

When you arrive at the airport, Terry Mills will get in touch with you. Terry is our on-site conference coordinator and will personally escort you to the Hospitality Hotel for check-in.

We feel that you know more about the flights you wish to use than we do, so we will leave reservations in your hands. As you know, we will reimburse you for tourist class travel, round trip between your home and Miami, and for ground transportation in your own city. You can submit the airfare and ground costs with the billing for your professional fee.

We are delighted that you will be speaking at our annual conference in Miami next month. I wanted to let you know as soon as possible about the arrangements for your trip.

All the food expenses in Miami will be taken care of for you. Luncheons are buffets in the ballroom — you can just go in and help yourself. When you register at the hotel you will receive tickets for dinner on the day of your presentation. Just sign your breakfast bills so we can pay them with your hotel bill.

Please phone me collect if you have any unanswered questions, or if we have forgotten some detail. You can reach me at (505) 444-8881, extension 11.

Question: What type of organization did you use?

Answer and suggested revision of letter can be found in the Appendix, page 301.

Writing can proceed much more easily if writers understand the phases in the writing process: (1) planning, (2) drafting, and (3) editing. Each phase should be distinct and separate. During the *planning* stage, the writer must understand the purpose, the audience or reader, and the subject of the document. To make sure you understand the purpose, get as much guidance as possible in the beginning of your project.

Readers can be categorized according to their roles: managers, experts or advisors, operators, and general readers or laypersons. For each of these categories of readers, you need to determine the decision-making level, knowledge of the subject, type or form of information needed, and likely reaction to what you write. If you are writing for a diverse audience, you need to speak to both primary and secondary readers. To understand your subject, make sure you collect and analyze relevant information.

Once you have determined your purpose, audience, and subject, you are ready to produce an outline. You may start with a non-linear form, then determine relationships and order of topics. Once you do that, you are ready to create a formal or semiformal outline. This is a "working outline," which you may want to change as you draft your document.

---

[1]*Using Writer-Friendly Documents.* <www.plainlanguage.gov>, p. 3.

[2]Lindsell-Roberts, Sheryl. *Business Writing for Dummies.* New York: IDG Books Worldwide, 1999, p. 19.

[3]*Using Writer-Friendly Documents.* <www.plainlanguage.gov>, p. 7.

[4]Piotrowski, Maryann V. *Effective Business Writing: A Guide for Those Who Write on the Job.* New York: HarperCollins, 1996, pp. 7-8.

[5]Pfeiffer, William S. *Pocket Guide to Technical Writing.* New York: IDG Books, 1999, pp. 9-10. Also see Monroe, Judson. *Effective Research and Report Writing in Government.* New York: McGraw-Hill, 1980, pp. 245-246.

CHAPTER 3

Drafting: Writing It Down

Getting It Down on Paper

Tom began to write the first draft of his recommendation of Marcia Smith. One of his paragraphs read as follows:

> I have always been impressed by Marcia's thoroughness, adherence to quality, and honesty. Her honesty extends from areas where we easily see it (in relationships and business transactions) to integrity of thought. Scientific, thorough, and meticulous, she approaches any analytical task with an exacting eye. This is what I mean by integrity of thought. She also is helpful and pleasant to work with, in fact, she takes the time to help those who are learning their way.

"What do you think of this paragraph?" Tom asked his colleague, Bob.

"Well, it has some good points," Bob said. "You explained what you meant by honesty and provided good examples of Marcia's honesty. Also, you have varied sentence structure. Some of your sentences are long and some are short. One of them begins with a phrase ("Scientific, thorough, and meticulous") instead of the standard subject-verb format.

"However, I would change a couple of things. I think you try to cover too many topics in this paragraph. It does not seem unified. Perhaps you could discuss only Marcia's honesty in this paragraph and discuss her helpfulness in another. Also, you have a run-on sentence. You need to put a period or semicolon after 'pleasant to work with.'"

"Hey, thanks so much," Tom said. "You've been really helpful."

Chapter 2 focused on how to organize your writing in a general way. Now that you know what you're going to write, the ideas to include, and the order in which to include them, it's time to put your plan into action.

This case study illustrates two important features of a first draft: paragraphs and sentences. This chapter will discuss how to organize the paragraphs and structure the sentences in your writing.

TURNING OFF YOUR INNER CRITIC

Remember, you are writing your *first draft*. You are not aiming to produce a perfect document on the first try. If you attempt to do so, you may find yourself facing paralysis and frustration, because you are trying to do two very different things at once: write and edit. So turn off the your inner critic and give your creative self the freedom to write without constraint.

Plunge into your first draft with the goal of getting something down on paper—or on your computer screen. Leave concerns about tone, word choice, spelling, and grammar to the editing stage. You can go back and correct your grammar, spelling, and sentence structure later. Right now, the most important thing is to get into the flow of writing. If you cannot think of a particular word to use, leave it blank. You can always add it later.

GETTING STARTED ON YOUR FIRST DRAFT

Deborah Dumaine recommends three steps to take in moving from your outline to your first draft:

1. Take each topic in your outline and create a headline for it. Begin with the topic that you feel most comfortable with. You do not need to write your first draft in order.

2. Take each headline and write a paragraph for it. The headline becomes the topic sentence of the paragraph.

3. Add new headlines as you need them, then write the paragraphs to go with them.[1]

Use whatever writing technique is easiest for you. For example, you might try one of the following:

- Set your timer and start writing. Write as quickly as you can, sticking to the ideas in your outline.

- Go to the outline (list of headlines) in your computer. Write a paragraph for each in any order. Then print out what you have drafted to see how it looks on paper.

- If speaking is easier than writing for you, try dictating your first draft. Then type up what you have written to see how it looks.[2]

PLANNING PARAGRAPHS

Paragraphs are groups of related sentences set off as distinct sections. They serve several purposes. A well-written paragraph helps the reader by breaking down complex ideas into manageable parts, focusing attention on one idea at a time, and relating each part to the main idea of the document. Paragraphs focus attention on important points. They also give variety to your page by breaking up long blocks of text.

A well-developed paragraph does not need to be long. *Paragraphs should be long enough to make their point adequately—and no longer.* The trend today is toward shorter paragraphs, just as it is toward shorter sentences. Use your eye to monitor paragraph length. If a paragraph turns a page into a mass of gray, find a way to break it into shorter paragraphs. If your paragraph is more than 10–12 lines (about 2 inches), you should consider breaking it into two or more paragraphs, even if it develops a single idea. Many writers recommend that paragraphs be no longer than 5–6 lines.

Using the headline-writing technique will help you get started on writing paragraphs.

QUALITIES OF EFFECTIVE PARAGRAPHS

Effective paragraphs have several characteristics:

1. **Unity:** Each element of the paragraph contributes to the main idea; nothing irrelevant appears.

2. **Coherence:** The parts of the paragraph relate clearly to each other, with each element leading logically to the next.

3. **Development:** The main idea is well supported with details—facts, examples, and reasons.

Unity

The writers of *Using Reader-Friendly Documents* say this about paragraphing:

> Limiting each paragraph to one issue gives the document a clean appearance and contributes to the impression that it is easy to read and understand.[3]

Limiting each paragraph to one topic also is a way of making sure that the reader doesn't miss or confuse your main points. Tacking on a second idea at the end of a paragraph, or burying one in the middle, can have three negative consequences:

- The reader may fail to grasp the importance of the second idea.

- The reader may be distracted from the first idea, which is the actual topic of the paragraph.

- The reader may get the impression that your thinking is muddled.

The Need for a Topic Sentence

The *topic sentence* summarizes and introduces what a paragraph is all about. You can think of a paragraph as a symphony movement; the topic sentence is the major theme and the rest of the paragraph is the development of that theme.

Your reader is usually best served if you put the topic sentence first in the paragraph. This practice shortens reading time. The reader does not have to look through the paragraph to find its main point. Also, the reader can skim the topic sentences of all the paragraphs to get the gist of the entire document. Again, think of the inverted pyramid. Put the most important information on top.

Consider the following example:

> We have two criteria for the equipment: economy and size. It is necessary that the equipment be economical; we cannot invest more than $200. It is also important that it fit into the space we have available—2 feet by 3 feet by 3 feet.

Here the main criteria for the equipment are stated in a topic sentence at the outset of the paragraph. Then the body of the paragraph explains why these criteria are being used and specifies them in dollars and space.

In some cases, it may not be best to put the topic sentence first. For example, you might want to begin your paragraph with a transition sentence that ties the paragraph to the preceding one. In these cases, the topic sentence should be the second sentence.

Also, putting the topic sentence later in the paragraph is sometimes better when you have to convey bad news. This indirect approach prepares the reader for the unpleasantness. In most situations, however, it is best to say what you have to say first and explain it later.

How to Develop the Topic Sentence

If you have already written a paragraph and need to create a topic sentence for it, you might take this approach:

1. Identify the main idea of your paragraph. Ask yourself, "What am I trying to say in this paragraph?"

2. Write down a headline sentence—the simplest form of your main idea that you can think of.

3. Write the entire sentence by answering the following questions:

   —Who?

   —What?

   —When?

   —Where?

   —Why?

   —How?

4. Refer to the headline whenever you need to.

The following is an example of how to do this:

Headline: Taxes are due.

Question: What kind of taxes?

Sentence: Corporation taxes are due.

Question: When?

Sentence: Corporation taxes are due within 60 days of fiscal closing.

Question: Why? (or, Under what conditions?)

Sentence: Due to a new regulation governing the timing of tax payments, corporation taxes are now due within 60 days of fiscal closing.[4]

In developing the paragraph, you may need to do the work in two stages:

1. Put down your thoughts in the order that they come to you.

2. Change that order.

Here is a paragraph that reflects the flow of its writer's initial thinking process:

> The ADSI 1000 Electronic Printing System consists of an input subsystem, either a tape transport for off-line printing or an interface unit for on-line operations, a control subsystem for processing and displaying and storing digital data, a subsystem that produces the image, and the output subsystem that routes sheets to an output

stacker bin at the rate of three sheets per second. It should be noted that this rate is 50 percent faster than that of the ADSI's nearest competitor. In fact, the ADSI is the fastest system of its kind on the market.

The writer's main point—the selling point—appears all the way at the bottom of the paragraph instead of at the top; the writer has worked up to it. To be effective, the paragraph needs to be turned around so that it starts off with this main point:

The ADSI is the fastest system of its kind on the market—50% faster than its nearest competitor.

The following are examples of effective topic sentences:

- Ginnie Maes can provide worry-free investment income.

- Capital spending increased dramatically in November.

- The new software program provides three major benefits.

Coherence

A paragraph is coherent if the reader can see how it holds together without having to puzzle out the writer's reasons for adding each new sentence. Within a paragraph, as within an entire written message, there should be a logical movement or progression.

Expressing Elements of a Paragraph Consistently

Your paragraph will be more coherent if you maintain the same person and tense throughout the paragraph.

- **Person.** Switching from "you" to "one" to "he" can be very disconcerting to the reader, as the following example illustrates:

  > For example, if you are a law student, you may already know that you want a job with a corporate law firm. Those who are business students may know that their aim is to enter executive training programs as the first step in retailing careers. If the person is getting an advanced degree in art history, however, he or she may be somewhat less clear about their goal.

- **Tense.** Maintain the same tense for the same subject within a paragraph; for example, events in the past should not be described in the present and also in the past tense. Use the present tense whenever you can.

  If the events you are discussing have taken place over a period of time, use a sequence of tenses to make the time relationships clear.

  Confusing*:*
  If your time log has shown that most of your interruptions were from people around you, obviously you are not going to be able to solve the problem by controlling incoming calls.

  Better*:*
  If your time log shows that most of your interruptions are from people around you, obviously you can't solve the problem by controlling incoming calls.

Using Transitional Devices for Continuity
Conjunctions (such as "and," "but," and "or") and *transition words* (such as "therefore" and "however") help readers

follow the flow of ideas in a paragraph—or between paragraphs. The following are some relationships and the transition words that can express them:

- *Contrast*—however, although, but, conversely, nevertheless, yet, still, on the other hand, even so, even though, in contrast, in spite of, on the contrary, regardless, otherwise

- *Comparison*—similarly, likewise, in the same way

- *Cause and effect*—as a result, therefore, consequently, thus, so, because

- *Example*—for instance, for example, specifically, as an illustration

- *Addition*—moreover, besides, in addition, also, too, furthermore

- *Time*—now, later, after, before, meanwhile, following, then

- *Sequence*—first, second, third, next, last, finally

- *Place*—further on, above, below, nearly, on the left, behind, around

- *Repetition or summation*—all in all, in conclusion, in summary, in other words.

Use Reference Words and Repetition for Linkage

Use reference words like "this," "that," "these," "those," and other demonstrative pronouns to tie in new ideas with points made earlier. Also, link your ideas by repeating the topic or key words. For example, if you are writing a report on the benefits of a software program, you might repeat the word "benefit" in each paragraph as a cue to the reader that you are continuing the main idea.

Development

A paragraph may be both unified and coherent but still be inadequate. This is because some writers fail to substantiate ideas with supporting facts and explanations. Their readers become interested in the subject, only to be disappointed when no further information is provided. Other writers get so carried away with a subject that they give too much information and bore their readers.

You need to find a way to develop your ideas adequately, but not excessively.

A well-developed paragraph provides the specific information that readers need and expect to understand you and to stay interested in what you are saying. You may want to develop and arrange the information according to a specific pattern.

The patterns of paragraph development are similar to those for overall development of your document. The following are some of these patterns:

- *Chronological or sequential* (first, next, last). Especially useful when explaining procedures, spelling out an action plan, or narrating a sequence of events.

- *Geographical* (north to south, basement to top floor, etc.). Useful when describing or analyzing an organization's activity, area by area.

- *Size* (largest to smallest, or smallest to largest). Useful in explaining some procedures, or in selling some ideas for change.

- *Familiar to unfamiliar.* Helpful when explaining new ideas or procedures, or when selling an idea that may threaten the reader (if only because it is new and different).

- *Most acceptable to least acceptable.* Useful when you know or can predict what the reader is likely to accept or reject.

- *General to specific.* Useful when you want to (1) state a principle and then give examples, or (2) state a rule and then give exceptions. You make the general statement and follow it with specific examples, limitations, qualifications, exclusions, or modifications.

TEST YOURSELF: ORGANIZING PARAGRAPHS

A. Putting the Main Idea Up Front; Cutting Ideas that Don't Belong

Read over the seven sentences that follow. Then decide how you would make a unified, well-planned paragraph out of them.

1. Two of the sentences do not contribute to the topic being discussed. Cross them out.

2. The remaining five sentences can be rearranged to form a coherent paragraph. Decide how you would arrange them to put the main idea up front and give the paragraph a logical order of development. Number the sentences 1 to 5, with the topic sentence as number 1, the next sentence as number 2, and so on.

   — One way to practice is selecting a subject in your spare moments and making yourself say something about it as quickly as possible.

— Once you have decided on a subject, you can discipline yourself to pull your thoughts together and commence your own statement on the subject within seconds.

— Failure to hold up your end of a conversation may be seen as impolite.

— The subjects may come from newspaper headlines, magazine contents, book or chapter titles, and overheard remarks.

— Perhaps the most important thing to be said about conversation is that practice is essential to improvement and that you can practice on your own without waiting for an audience to come along.

— Sometimes you will continue to talk spontaneously on the subject until you run out of material; at other times you may set a goal of talking for two or three minutes.

— The best time to practice may be when you get up in the morning.

B. Making New Paragraphs

Expressed in a single paragraph, the material that follows looks massive and uninviting. How would you break it up into four paragraphs? Indicate where you would make the paragraph breaks by inserting paragraph symbols (¶).

A process is any series of actions in a sequence that brings about a particular result or condition. Studying is a process. So is driving a car, getting dressed, doing research, manufacturing something, or performing a laboratory experiment. Processes include not only fairly simple procedures, methods, techniques, and activities, but also complex ones. A process can be described as a series of continuous actions from (1) the point of view of an observer or onlooker, or (2) the point of view of the participant or doer of the actions. If the purpose is merely to inform the reader, the process is described from the point of view of the observer. If the purpose is to give instructions to someone who is to perform the process, the description of the process should be written from the point of view of a participant. The two viewpoints, however, should never be mixed in describing a particular process. To mix the two would confuse the reader completely. Regardless of which viewpoint is used, it often is necessary to include illustrations. Such illustrations may include photographs, drawings, flow charts, graphs, tables, diagrams, or schematics as needed to show individual actions in sequence. When describing and explaining a process it is usually desirable to follow a fairly well standardized pattern—one that has become standardized not because of arbitrary considerations but because it leads to explanations that are easy to understand. This pattern calls for an introduction, an overall picture including a list of the main steps that make up the process, an explanation of each step listed, and a conclusion if it seems that one would be helpful.

Answers can be found in the Appendix, page 302.

TEST YOURSELF: WRITING TOPIC SENTENCES

In the space at the top of each of the following paragraphs, add a topic sentence:

_____

_____

1. The first element is known as unity; it says that each element of the paragraph will contribute to the main idea, that nothing irrelevant will appear. A second element is coherence. This simply means that one element leads logically to the next. Finally, the good paragraph is adequately developed; there are enough details to make the main point clear.

---

2. The four years of experience may seem a great deal, but we have found that successful planners do have this much related experience behind them; people with less experience just don't seem to work out. We would consider waiving the college degree for a candidate who had at least two years of college and extra related experience with another agency. Skill in interpersonal relations is a must.

Answer can be found in the Appendix, page 304.

WRITING SENTENCES

Whenever you express a complete thought or feeling, naming something and telling something about it, you are writing a **sentence**. In its simplest form, a sentence has two essential elements: a subject and a predicate.

The subject is who or what the sentence is about. Sometimes the subject of a sentence is *implied* rather than actually *stated*. In giving instructions, for example, you might say, "Turn left at the end of the hall." What you are really saying is, "You turn left at the end of the hall." The "you" is implied. Note that many of the sentences in this handbook, including this one, are written in this way.

The predicate is the part of the sentence that says something about the subject. For example, in the sentence, "The Computer Support Department looks forward to providing network assistance to the agency," the predicate is "looks forward to providing network assistance to the agency."

Sentence Fragments

Sentences must be complete. A *sentence fragment* is a part of a sentence that is set off as if it were a whole sentence. Unlike a complete sentence, a sentence fragment lacks a subject, a predicate, or both, or it is a subordinate clause not attached to a complete sentence.

Fragment: Your salary.   (lacks a predicate)

Fragment: Will be increased.   (lacks a subject)

Sentence: Your salary will be increased.

Fragment: After your salary is increased. (is a subordinate clause)

Sentence: After your salary is increased, you will feel more content.

Run-on Sentences

Careless writers often fall into another kind of error with sentences. They write *run-on sentences*, in which two main clauses are joined by only a comma with no connecting word.

"Meet me at the office at nine, I'll be waiting for you."

"There are those who will tell you my job is easy, don't believe them, they are talking sheer nonsense."

Those sentences are incorrect. The following are examples of correct versions of each:

"Meet me at the office at nine. I'll be waiting for you."

"There are those who will tell you my job is easy. Don't believe them. They are talking sheer nonsense."

Overloaded Sentences

The following sentence is not, strictly speaking, grammatically incorrect. But it does impede the reader's understanding by piling up too many ideas, one after the other.

The statements were made by Richard N. Wilson, Project Director for the Southern Regional Center, a federally funded, department-sponsored project that does research for participating agencies in Region IV, a region which includes Kentucky, Tennessee, North Carolina, South Carolina, Georgia, Alabama, Mississippi, and Florida.

TEST YOURSELF: OVERLOADED SENTENCES

How would you rewrite the previous sentence to make it clearer? *(Answer can be found in the Appendix, page 304.)*

The authors of NPR's *Writing User-Friendly Documents* say the following about sentence length:

Express only one idea in each sentence. Long, complicated sentences often mean that you aren't clear about what you want to say. Shorter sentences show clear thinking. Shorter sentences are also better for conveying complex information; they break the information up into smaller, easier-to-process units. Vary your sentences to avoid choppiness, but don't revert to multi-clause sentences.[5]

Choppy Sentences

Barbara Fine Clouse gives an example of choppy sentences:

> Read this paragraph out loud. It sounds choppy. The style seems immature. The writing does not sound like it was written by a forty-two-year-old woman with a couple of college degrees. It sounds like it was written by someone's kid brother.[6]

Contrast this with the following paragraph:

> If you read this paragraph out loud, you'll realize that it sounds choppy. The style seems immature, as though it were written by someone's kid brother, rather than by a forty-two-year-old woman with a couple of college degrees.

To overcome choppiness, try the following:

- Use different sentence openers. The paragraph above sounds choppy because most of the sentences begin with the subject. To alleviate this repetitious pattern, try one of the following suggestions:

  —Open with a descriptive word (a modifier). "Strangely, the government did not give liberal leave during last week's snow storm."

  —Open with a descriptive phrase (a modifier). "Despite my better judgment, I let Harold take over the project."

  —Open with a subordinate clause (a dependent word group with a subject and verb). "When Congress announced its budget reform package, members of both political parties offered their support."

—Open with an infinitive ("to" plus a verb). "To protect our resources, we must make recycling a way of life."

- Vary the placement of transitions (words and phrases that link ideas).

  —In addition, providing child care in the workplace is a good idea because half of all mothers work. (*transition at the beginning*)

  —Jan's opinion, on the other hand, is that child-care programs will cost too much money. (*transition in the middle*)

  —Many employers now offer day care as a benefit, however. (*transition at the end*)

- Combine short sentences.

  The Recreation Division will close its Central City offices next fall. The closing will occur because of downsizing.

  Next fall, because of downsizing, the Recreation Division will close its Central City offices.

- Vary the length of your sentences.

  (*Example*) This office needs a director who knows how to deal effectively with upper management and how to trim waste from the budget. This office needs Lee Johnson.

- Use your ear. Read your paragraphs aloud. When you hear that the sentences are not flowing well, place a check mark. Then go back and use the techniques just described to ease the flow.[7]

TEST YOURSELF: SOUND SENTENCES

A. Some of the following sentences are complete. Others are run-on sentences, while others are sentence fragments. In front of the number for each sentence, put the symbol that applies:

C   for complete sentence
R   for run-on sentence
F   for sentence fragment

1. Although you argued with me.

2. Because my friend likes movies, we often go to the theater, we go to concerts, too.

3. You may have the book; I have finished it.

4. Never in my life had I seen such a mess.

5. The team, going around in circles, trying to get the project done before the next deadline stared them in the face.

6. He went to the meeting?

7. Since you are unwilling to accept the offer, we will have to look for another candidate.

8. Try to use the manual, you will find it very simple, I assure you.

9. That's good.

10. Hoping to hear from you soon.

B. Make complete sentences out of these fragments:

1. While we are on the subject.

2. To the files.

3. Feeling lost, the new employee in my office.

C. Insert or substitute proper punctuation to remedy these run-on sentences.

1. You don't have to be concerned about it, I'll take care of it.

2. On the one hand, we can take the positive view and hope the problem solves itself, on the other hand, we can take action to solve it immediately.

3. There are two methods of sampling, they are the simple random sample method (which assigns each individual name a number and then draws numbers) and the area sampling method (which selects city blocks of individuals).

Answers can be found in the Appendix, page 304.

TEST YOURSELF: REWRITING TOM'S LETTER

Re-read the case study at the beginning of this chapter. Take the suggestions given by Bob and rewrite Tom's paragraph.

A suggested paragraph is given in the Appendix, page 305.

TIPS FOR WRITING YOUR DRAFT

Pfeifffer recommends the following:

- Once you have a complete outline in hand, write your first draft quickly.

- Schedule blocks of drafting time. Do whatever is needed to prevent being interrupted for at least 30 to 60 minutes.

- Don't stop to edit.

- Begin with the easiest section.

- Write summaries last.[8]

HOW TO AVOID WRITER'S BLOCK

You may find that you become stuck while writing your first draft. You may reach a point where you cannot seem to go on. To avoid wasting time during this stage of the writing process, try these tips:

1. Change your environment—find a quiet place with no distractions.

2. Take a break and come back to your task refreshed.

3. Start writing the section of the document that comes most easily or, depending on your makeup, the section that is most difficult. In either case, do not feel you must write down your ideas in the order in which they will ultimately appear.

4. If possible, avoid writing when you are emotionally or mentally preoccupied or physically fatigued.

5. Find the time of day and the place that you do your best writing.

6. Promise yourself a reward for your hard work.

GETTING SOME DISTANCE FROM YOUR DRAFT

After you finish writing your first draft, walk away from it. It's difficult to be objective when you are too close to your writing. In a perfect world, you have the time to put your draft aside and revisit it in a day or two—but this is not a perfect world, and we seldom have the time to do this. However, even a 10- to 15-minute break can make a difference. When you're pressed for time, try one of the following:

- Try to clear your mind for a few moments. Visualize the site of your last vacation.

- Go for a short walk—even if it's just down the hall and back.

- Get a cup of coffee.

- Make a quick telephone call about a completely different project.

REVISITING THE DRAFT

After you get some distance, it's time to be more critical. Then you can look at the overall draft and check a few things *before* going into the editing stage. Take a minute to assess the following:

☑ Did I explain my purpose clearly?

☑ Did I consider the role, knowledge level, attitude, and other characteristics of the reader?

☑ Does the overall organization of the draft make sense?

☑ Did I provide closure? (For example, did you tell readers exactly what you want them to do?)

During the drafting stage, it is important to work quickly and freely and to let your ideas flow. This means resisting any temptation to edit as you write.

During this stage, you want to focus on paragraphing—making sure that your paragraphs are unified, coherent, and well developed. You also want to look at your sentences to make sure they are correct, concise, and smooth.

During the drafting stage, you may find yourself at an impasse. Writers frequently experience this feeling of "writer's block," and deal with it in a variety of ways.

After you have completed the draft, get some distance before looking at it critically. After taking a cursory look at your first draft, you are ready to go on to the editing stage.

---

[1]Dumaine, Deborah. *Write to the Top: Writing for Corporate Success.* New York: Random House, 1989, pp. 77-78.

[2]Dumaine, Deborah. *Write to the Top: Writing for Corporate Success.* New York: Random House, 1989, pp. 60-62.

[3]*Using Writer-Friendly Documents.* <www.plainlanguage.gov>, p. 3.

[4]Adapted from Monroe, Judson, *Effective Research and Report Writing in Government.* New York: McGraw-Hill, 1980.

[5]*Using Writer-Friendly Documents.* <www.plainlanguage.gov>, p. 4.

[6]Clouse, Barbara Fine. *Working It Out: A Troubleshooting Guide for Writers.* Second Ed. New York: McGraw-Hill, 1997, p. 90.

[7]Ibid., pp. 91-93.

[8]Pfeiffer, William S. *Pocket Guide to Technical Writing.* New York: IDG Books, 1999, pp. 12-13.

CHAPTER 4

Editing: Using the Right Voice and Tone

Setting the Tone

"I have a draft of a proposed regulation for you to read," said Lee, Jane's co-worker. "It just doesn't sound right. Perhaps you can offer some suggestions."

Jane sat down and read the following document:

It has been noted that employees in this agency are spending excessive amounts of time on the Internet during regular working hours. This practice has been observed to have increased in the past year. All employees need to stop this practice immediately or severe measures will be taken. If any part of this message is not clear, please call the Director's office and it will be explained.

"You can improve this in two ways," Jane told Lee. "First, try to use a friendlier tone. Then, change the passive voice to active voice."

Lee came back a little later and showed Jane the following revised regulation:

We'd like to ask your cooperation in helping to make our agency more productive. Please limit your use of the Internet to searches that are directly related to your job. In addition, please try to make Internet searches efficient. Schedule specific amounts of time for yourself—preferably no more than a half-hour at a time.

While the Internet is a valuable tool for research and communication, it can also be a distraction. If you have any questions about Internet use, please call the Director's office.

"That's a great improvement," said Lee. "Now maybe they won't feel like throwing things at us."

Now that you have words on paper, it's time to edit your work. You may not be able to send your writing to the copy desk, but you can turn a critical eye on yourself. The best plan is to put your first draft away for a while before beginning to edit it. This allows you to look at it from a fresh perspective. Or, ask someone whose writing you admire to look it over.

As you can see from the scenario just described, voice and tone can either strengthen or weaken the impact of writing. Using the active voice, selecting strong verbs, and deciding on the right tone can make a world of difference in your business writing. In this chapter, you'll learn how to recognize and correct problems in these areas.

WRITING TIP: PREFER THE ACTIVE VOICE

We often lessen the impact of our writing by using the passive voice.

In an active sentence, the person or agency performing an action is the subject of the sentence. In a passive sentence, the person or item that is acted upon is the subject of the sentence.

Changing passive voice to active voice in your writing can add energy and cut wordiness. As noted in *Writing User-Friendly Documents,* "More than any other writing technique, using active voice and specifying who is taking an action will change the character of our writing."[1]

How to Recognize Passive and Active Sentences

The active voice emphasizes who is doing something:

"The Personnel Department will document the procedures next week."

The actor (the Personnel Department) comes first in the sentence. That actor, the subject of the sentence, does the action.

The passive voice shows who or what is being acted upon:

"The procedures will be documented by the Personnel Department next week."

Passive sentences have two basic features, though they do not occur in every passive sentence:

- Some form of the verb "to be" as a helping verb

- A past participle (generally with "ed" on the end).

Passive voice:

"The checks *have been* mailed."

"Regulations *have been proposed* by the Department of Veterans Affairs."

"You *were asked* by me."

"Copies *are prepared* downstairs."

Active voice:

"We *mailed* the checks."

"We *have proposed* regulations."

"I *asked* you."

"Mark and Susan *prepare* copies downstairs."

Often the word "by" appears after the verb to show who performs the action of the verb.

Passive voice: "The speech was given *by* the director."

Active voice: "The director gave the speech."

The Case for the Active Voice

You should use the active rather than the passive voice for most sentences. As a rule, if you rewrite a passive sentence to make it active, the sentence will read better.

There are several reasons for choosing the active voice:

1. A sentence with an active verb form sounds more natural; the active voice is the way we usually think.

    Passive: "The meal was enjoyed by us."

    Active: "We enjoyed the meal."

2. The active voice is more vigorous and direct. The passive voice makes writing weak.

    Passive: "An excellent job was done by Stacy."

    Active: "Stacy did an excellent job."

    Passive: "Many complaints are heard about the working conditions."

    Active: "Many people are complaining about the working conditions."

3. The passive voice can be confusing, especially in sentences like this one:

    Passive: "A survey was made by the Department of Health of the screening clinic at University Hospital."

    Who is doing what? In the active voice, all doubts are removed.

> *Active*:   "The Department of Health surveyed the screening clinic at University Hospital."

4. The passive voice adds length to writing. Look back over the samples. In each case, the sentence in the active voice is shorter than the sentence in the passive voice.

5. Sentences with active verbs make the writer seem confident; sentences with passive verbs sound evasive, show an unwillingness to accept or assign responsibility, and often give less information.

> *Passive*:   "The decision was made to eliminate employee bonuses."

> *Active*:   "The president decided to eliminate employee bonuses."

The Case for the Passive Voice

The passive voice can be used occasionally:

1. When one action follows another as a matter of law, and there is no actor (besides the law itself) for the second action

   Passive: "If you do not pay the royalty on your mineral production, your lease will be terminated [by the action of the law]."[2]

2. To move the important element to the front of the sentence where it will have greater prominence than in the middle or at the end

   Passive: "The President was released from the hospital."

   Passive: "Any employee who violates this policy will be terminated."

3. To point out an error or shortcoming in a diplomatic way

   Passive: "An error was made in the last set of calculations."

   Passive: "Some phases of the study were done perfunctorily at best, negligently at worst. "

4. In cases when the agents performing the action are unknown, unidentifiable, or unimportant

   Passive: "Traffic was brought to a standstill."

   Passive: "It has been shown that people tend to look away while they are speaking."

How to Activate Passive Sentences

To change passive sentences to active, follow these three steps:

1. Find or supply the actor (s).

   "An excellent job was done by Stacy." *Stacy* is the actor.

2. Put the actor in front of the sentence.

   "Stacy . . .

3. Replace the passive verb with an active verb.

   "Stacy did an excellent job."

To communicate effectively, write the majority of your sentences in the active voice.

TEST YOURSELF: GIVING SENTENCES ACTION BY CHANGING PASSIVE TO ACTIVE VOICE

Rewrite the following sentences. Change passive voice to active voice. Say things as directly as you can. Supply the subject of the sentence when necessary.

1. Your patience is appreciated.

2. Exercises are provided in each chapter.

3. We hope that this matter will be promptly resolved by you.

4. A new machine is required for this section.

5. Our recommendations are summarized in this chart.

6. The assignment was transferred to me last week by my boss.

7. We are trying to bite off more than can be chewed.

8. When the alarm sounds, a shutdown of the machine must be effected at once.

9. This survey has been completed by all department heads.

10. Negotiations between the contractor and us have been held several times.

11. The conclusion has been reached that this process should not be changed.

12. A signed contract with an agency is required if you want to hire a temporary worker.

Answers can be found in the Appendix, page 306.

WRITING TIP: BRING SUBMERGED ACTION TO THE SURFACE

Verbs give action to sentences. Submerged verbs are those combined with auxiliary or other weak verbs and turned into nouns. Submerged verbs often occur in connection with the weak verbs "to be," "to make," and "to do."

Weak: "These changes will make our process more streamlined."

Stronger: "These changes will streamline our process."

Weak: "I will do interviews with the affected parties."

Stronger: "I will interview the affected parties."

Weak: "This report is intended to summarize our findings."

Stronger: "This report summarizes our findings."

Other weak verb forms may also submerge the action.

Weak: "He offered a proposed solution to the problem."

Stronger: "He proposed a solution."

Weak: "Stabilization of the compound took place early in the experiment."

Stronger: "The compound stabilized early in the experiment."

In the weak versions, the action has disappeared because the writer has turned the action verb into a noun.

Sometimes, using gerunds brings the action to the surface. (Gerunds are the noun/verb words ending in -*ing*.)

Submerged	*Surfaced*
by the use of the gerunds	by using gerunds
a resumption of operations will	resuming operations will
a reduction of costs can	reducing costs can

Note that each stronger or surfaced example is shorter than its weak or submerged counterpart.

TEST YOURSELF: BRINGING SUBMERGED VERBS TO THE SURFACE

Rewrite the following sentences. Change passive voice to active voice. Bring the submerged verbs to the surface. Say things as directly as you can. You'll find you can eliminate many words in the process.

1. These charts were developed to depict the results of our survey.

2. It is our recommendation that these findings be investigated.

3. Management example exerts a powerful influence on employee behavior.

4. These reports are an explanation of our findings.

5. My boss accomplished the transfer of responsibility to me last week.

6. We are of the opinion that these changes would be too costly.

7. When the red light gives an indication that the machine is overheating, shut it off.

8. An analysis has been made of that report.

9. We have made a thorough evaluation of your proposal.

10. After conducting a careful review of the evidence, we decided that there would be no justification for any further pursuit of this matter.

11. The accomplishment of the temporary reassignment of an employee requires a transfer arrangement.

12. The confirmation of the contract occurred yesterday.

Answers can be found in the Appendix, page 307.

WRITING TIP: SUBSTITUTE ACTION VERBS FOR FORMS OF "TO BE"

Forms of "to be" (am, is, are, was, were) have less energy and interest than action verbs do. Whenever possible, opt for action verbs.

Less energy: My boss *was* always a believer in empowerment.

More energy: My boss always *believed* in empowerment.

Trying to avoid forms of the verb "to be" may even force you to become creative and descriptive:

Less energy: After the office social, people *were* happier.

More energy: After the office party, people *smiled*, *chatted*, and *thanked* the members of the Social Committee.

CHOOSING YOUR WORDS: TONE IN WRITING

Tone reflects the way you sound on paper, the way you convey an attitude or mood. As noted in *Writing User-Friendly Documents*, tone strongly affects your reader's reaction:

> Although you can't hear it, tone in a letter has much the same effect as it has when you speak to someone. What's your reaction when someone speaks to you in a cold tone? Do you tune out of the conversation; pay more attention to the tone than the content; or walk away? Readers do much the same thing. When the tone of a letter is cold or harsh, many times readers will put down the letter and pick up the telephone.[3]

We use some of the following words to describe tone:

- friendly
- personal
- indifferent
- angry
- annoying
- empathetic
- serious
- matter-of-fact.

Choose a tone that is appropriate to your particular reader, your purpose, and the subject matter.

Finding the Right Tone

The appropriate tone for most business writing conveys friendliness, concern, and respect—without being overly familiar or ingratiating, and without hedging.

Business writing is becoming more informal, friendly, and straightforward. Nevertheless, an element of judgment is usually involved in finding the right tone. You need to judge, for example, when a personal expression is just right—and when a reflection of your personality, opinions, and feelings would be distracting or embarrassing. You need to judge when you're being businesslike at the cost of being friendly.

Using an "Adult" Tone

In his book, *Games People Play,* Eric Berne describes a concept known as transactional analysis. According to this theory, the human personality is composed of three discrete elements called the *child,* the *parent,* and the *adult.* Any transaction, or contact between two people, is affected by the dominant element. The dominant element might be revealed in the tone of a memo or letter. For example, consider the following three statements:

1. If the people in the office weren't so noisy, I could get my work done without having to stay late every night. **Whiny tone, blaming others and playing for sympathy:** *child.*

2. If you would just plan a little better, you could get your work done on time. **I-told-you, do-it-right tone that a** *parent* **might use with an errant child.**

3. I suggest you close our office door when there's a distraction so that you won't be disturbed. **Offers a reasonable solution to the problem and sounds very** *adult.*[4]

Most people respond to reasonable, straightforward communication. When they are addressed as adults by adults, they react as adults should react. Keeping in mind the principles of transactional analysis, make sure your writing has an adult tone.

Ways to Find the Appropriate Tone

Finding the right tone is not always easy, but it helps to think from the standpoint of your reader. As Judy Tenney notes:

> Using plain language as a writer means thinking from the perspective of the reader. It means creating a partnership between writer and reader in which each person works at clear communication. Again, plain language means "you," "we," and "I" working together![5]

- *Use "you," "your," or "yours"* to address your reader personally and add immediacy to your letter or report. One of the worst tone offenders in government writing is to refer to people as if they were inanimate objects. Notice the difference between the two sentences below:

    1. The leg injury is disabling; therefore, the payee is entitled to benefits.

    2. We found that you have a disabling leg injury; therefore, you are entitled to benefits.

    The two changes to the second sentences are the use of "you" and the active voice.

- *Use "I"* or, if you are writing on behalf of your organization, *use "we."* Let the reader know that a human is writing, not a machine.

    "I look forward to meeting you soon."

    "We'll process your application within 30 days of receiving it."

- *Also use "I" to:*

  —Write in a less negative or accusatory tone

  —Soften the blow of unpleasant news.

The following table shows the contrast between the following statements using second person ("you") and those using first person ("I"). Note that the "I" statements are wordier. Sometimes you must use more words to convey the accurate meaning and the appropriate tone.

Second Person "You"	First Person "I"
You didn't write the memo in the correct format.	I'd like to spend some time with you going over our correspondence formats.
You were late coming back from lunch at 2:30 p.m.	I want to clarify our lunch-period policy. You must take your 30-minute lunch period between 11:30 a.m. and 2 p.m. We need everyone back at work by 2.
You must resubmit your request using the right form.	I can expedite your refund, so I'm enclosing Form 112E. Please fill it out, sign your full name on line 5, and return the form to me.
You miscalculated the total cost, and you owe us $243.	I recalculated the cost of your purchase based on the changes you requested. The total cost is now $943. I credited your deposit of $700 to your account, so the balance due to us is $243.

Second Person "You"	First Person "I"
You can't bring the class for a ride on NASA's shuttle.	Though I'm sorry we can't give Shuttle rides to your class, I'm enclosing a simulation video I'm sure they'll enjoy. I'm also sending along Space Camp applications for everyone.

- *Say "please," "thanks," and "thank you"* where appropriate.

  "Please send us a statement explaining why you reduced the number of your credit hours."

  "Thank you for sending us…"

- *Ask questions.*

  "May we have your reply by March 20?"

  "Have we failed to cover an important detail?"

  "What can we do to help?"

- *Use parentheses* to say "By the way," or "If you don't need this extra explanation or background, you can just skip to the end of the parentheses."

  "These forms must be prepared in duplicate (see the Regulations, Chapter 6, Paragraph 19) and submitted to…"

- *Use dashes* to signal "This is important."

  "We want to clear up this confusion—immediately."

  "Your remark raises a question—"Why?"—and that question is a good one."

- *Use italics,* ALL CAPS or *bold* type sparingly to emphasize points.

- *Use exclamation points with much restraint* in business writing—and in all your writing.

- *Use a sympathetic tone only when appropriate.* For instance, if you are writing to a widow who is asking questions about benefits, you may want to start the letter by saying: "We are sorry to hear about the death of your husband." If, however, this is the fourth letter you have sent to the same widow, don't just add the same line by rote.[6]

- When you have to communicate bad news or a disappointing response, try to put yourself in the reader's place. Try to *convey friendliness, concern, and warmth.* Or try to defuse the situation. Don't argue with the reader—just supply information needed to clarify points that may be confusing or misleading.

  Instead of: "You apparently misunderstood the requirements."

  Try: "Perhaps the requirements were not clear."

  Instead of: "You are not qualified for this benefit."

  Try: "Unfortunately, you do not qualify for this benefit."

- *Use "must" to indicate requirements.* The word "must" is the clearest way to convey to your readers what they have to do. Avoid using "shall" or "should."

  "You must file an appeal of the decision within 30 days."

- If you're saying no and asking for a response, be sure to *state the benefits of responding.*

  "We will forward your application as soon as we receive your check."

- If you're writing to complain, state facts and avoid emotion—which is not easy to do when you are angry. Probably the most effective approach is to *be firm and specific while keeping a sense of humor.*

- *If an apology is called for, make it*—without groveling or hedging. Apologize at once, for something specific, in as few words as possible.

  Instead of: "Rest assured that we deeply regret the inconvenience our error has possibly caused you."

  Try: "Thanks for informing us of the error. We hope you've not been inconvenienced by it."

- *Use the active voice.*

  Instead of: "An error was made in calculating your refund."

  Try: "We are sorry. We made a mistake when we calculated your refund."

- Where appropriate, *end on a positive note* by mentioning corrective action.

  "We're sending the balance of your refund today."

- Sometimes you need to qualify a statement; then, words such as "apparently" and "in general" have a place. But if you use such words habitually, your writing will have a hedging tone and imply that you aren't quite sure about what you're saying. *Here are some qualifying words and phrases to watch out for:*

apparently	in most cases
in general	seemingly
ordinarily	commonly
as a rule	it appears
in many instances	usually
seems to indicate	generally
as a usual case	normally

- *Use neutral or positive language* that puts the situation in the best light.

  Instead of: "Because your program failed four different evaluations..."

  Try: "Because evaluation requirements were not met..."

- *When you can convey good news, make it sound good.*

  Instead of: "This letter will inform you that you will be sponsored as this staff's representative to the annual meeting."

  Try: "Congratulations! Staff members have chosen you to represent them at the annual meeting."

- *Be sincere.* Don't gush. Don't lead the reader to question your credibility.

  Instead of: "The response was fantastic."

  Try: "Your idea received overwhelming support. The managers voted to feature it at the next staff meeting."

- *Don't make statements with a degree of certainty that is hardly appropriate.*

  "I am sure that you will agree that this arrangement is fair."

  "We are certain that you'll want to participate in this study."

- *Don't use superlatives* (words that identify the utmost degree) *when your statement cannot be backed up or proved.*

  "Our agency is the most efficient in the government."

"This camera is positively the best money can buy."

"We pay the highest interest rates available anywhere."

- *Don't draw conclusions for your readers* instead of letting them conclude for themselves.

"This indispensable guide represents a bargain for any busy administrator."

"Having assembled an outstanding team of researchers and designers, the contractor is fully prepared and uniquely qualified to accomplish the task."

- *Don't suggest surprise.*

"Your statement came as a great surprise to me."

"We cannot understand why you have not filled out the application."

"We wouldn't have thought it would take so long to repair the equipment."

- *Don't make it seem as if you're talking down to your reader.*

"You realize, obviously, that those results couldn't possibly be valid. It is well known, of course, that ... "

TEST YOURSELF: SAYING IT IN A FRIENDLIER WAY

Put yourself in the reader's place. Rewrite these lines to give them a tone you'd be more willing to hear.

1. Unfortunately, you wrote to the wrong department and your letter had to be rerouted.

2. If the points I've made aren't clear to you, you may call me during business hours.

3. Note that you need to sign the application before we can proceed.

4. As you failed to enclose a check, we cannot process your order.

5. The report you allegedly submitted on the 30th of last month has not arrived in this office.

6. We need to hear from you immediately regarding your decision on using the space.

7. This letter outlines steps to be taken by you in filing any claim.

8. Your request has been received and is being handled as expeditiously as possible.

9. We require your cooperation if this program is to be a success.

10. Fill out the form so that your opinion will be reflected in the survey.

11. The return of this report, after review, is requested.

12. If this change is desirable, it is necessary that the enclosed form be dated and signed.

Answers can be found in the appendix, page 308.

Voice and tone can either strengthen or weaken the impact of writing. Using the active voice, selecting strong verbs, and deciding on the appropriate tone can make a world of difference in your writing.

In an active sentence, the person or agency performing an action is the subject of the sentence, while in a passive sentence the person or item that is acted upon is the subject of the sentence. Although you may have occasion to use the passive voice, using the active voice in most of your writing will make your sentences sound more natural, direct, clear, and confident.

Make your writing stronger by selecting strong verbs. Use the verb "to be" only when necessary and avoid submerged verbs—those combined with auxiliary or other weak verbs and turned into nouns.

Finally, choose a tone that is both professional and friendly, and appropriate to your reader, your purpose, and the subject matter. To convey a friendlier tone, use "you," "we," and "I" whenever possible. Use "must" for requirements, and whether conveying good or bad news, keep your message sincere and positive. Use qualifying words and phrases sparingly, and make your apologies brief and specific.

---

[1]*Writing User-Friendly Documents.* <www.plainlanguage.gov>

[2]Ibid.

[3]Ibid.

[4]Berne, Eric. *Games People Play.* Ballantine Books. Reissue edition, 1996.

[5]Tenney, Judy. "Plain Language Means "You," "We," and "I" Working Together!" *Plain Language News,* <www.plainlanguage.gov/news/youme3.html.>

[6]*Writing User-Friendly Documents,* <www.plainlanguage.gov>

CHAPTER 5

Editing: *Writing with Clarity and Conciseness*

Jargon and "Gobbledygook"

Because Jane had done such a good job with her first writing assignment, her supervisor began asking her to review the writing of others—mainly staff. She found that the documents she was reviewing tended to have long and often confusing sentences. The writers tended to favor outdated expressions, such as "enclosed please find" and "we are in receipt of your application." They also used cumbersome phrases, such as "we deem it advisable" or "we will endeavor to ascertain." Jane found pretentious words, such as "promulgate" and "reside" sprinkled throughout the documents. Her goal was to make the letters and reports as clear and reader-friendly as possible.

When you edit your work, you want to make sure that your message is crystal clear and to the point. Your reader should not have to muddle through confusing, excess verbiage to discover the meaning. Readers who become frustrated by unclear writing may not read a document at all. What's the point of a regulation if the people it affects don't—or can't—read it? And what are the odds that people will comply with a regulation if they can't understand it?

PLAIN LANGUAGE AVOIDS LAWSUITS AND SAVES MONEY

As Mark R. Miller points out, unclear writing is more than annoying—some courts have called it unconstitutional. He notes the following:

A few years ago, the Immigration and Naturalization Service (INS) was taken to court by several aliens the INS had attempted to deport after they had failed to request hearings in document fraud cases. The INS had notified them of their right to request a hearing and informed them that, if they waived that right, they most likely would be deported.

The problem? The forms the INS used for notification were so unclear that the aliens didn't understand their rights or the possible legal consequences. The court not only ordered INS to rewrite the forms but also prevented the agency from deporting any alien who had received the forms.[1]

To avoid such problems, make sure your writing is understandable to anyone reading it. In this chapter, we show how to identify and correct unclear or wordy sentences.

Improved comprehension also saves regulators time and money. Joseph Kimble cites a 1991 study which showed that writing memos in plain language could save the U.S. Navy $250 to $350 million a year as a result of all naval personnel reading plain-language reports and memos instead of bureaucratic documents.[2]

The Veterans Benefits Administration (VBA) tracked the savings from rewriting just one letter in plain language. The letter, from the VBA's Insurance Service, asks insured veterans to update their beneficiary information. In the rewritten letter, the VBA presents information in a question- and-answer format and provides very direct and simply stated answers. Here's a before-and-after sample:

Before
"The proceeds of your life insurance policy will be paid to your last named beneficiary of record with the Department of Veterans Affairs according to the payment option selected by you. Our experience shows that many insureds

fail to keep their designations up-to-date when there are changes in their personal circumstances. . . . Therefore, if you desire, but have not selected the lump sum settlement option or cannot remember the option you selected, or believe your beneficiary designation is not otherwise current, we suggest you complete the enclosed form and return it to us."

After

"We are updating our computer systems for the year 2000. This also allows us to update the way we store our records and process our claims. This is a perfect opportunity for you to update your records as well. This letter will explain what we have done to update our records and what you can do to update yours."

The VBA projects that it will save more than $8 million because of this rewrite, as a result of decreased costs of tracking down beneficiaries to pay claims. This projection is based on a test mailing, which resulted in a 75% increase in the number of responses.

Examples of how the use of fewer words has resulted in reduced time and cost—and greater ease of public use—abound throughout the government. One outstanding example is Jane Virga of the Farm Credit Administration, who revised a document explaining the Freedom of Information Act fees. By the time she finished, the size of the document had shrunk from 7,850 to 4,018 words and still contained more information than the original.

Agencies have been cutting down on administrative costs, too. In the 1970s, the Federal Communications Commission rewrote in plain English the regulations for CB radios. The number of calls from people confused by the rules dropped so dramatically that the agency was able to reassign all five people who had been fielding questions full time.[3]

HOW TO IMPROVE CLARITY

You too can make your writing briefer and clearer. To reduce the number of words in your document, use shorter sentences, replace wordy expressions, and select shorter words.

Use Short Sentences

Many documents are never read or understood because of long, confusing sentences. Short sentences:

- Show clear thinking

- Break information into smaller, easier-to-process units

- Add vigor and clarity to your documents

- Help you translate complicated provisions into understandable language

- Hold the reader's interest.

The following is an example of a complex sentence that was divided into four shorter, clearer sentences:

Before:	*After:*
For good reasons, the Secretary may grant extensions of time in 30-day increments for filing of the lease and all required bonds, provided that additional extension requests are submitted and approved before the expiration of the original 30 days or the previously granted extension.	We may extend the time you have to file the lease and required bonds. Each extension will be granted for a 30-day period. To get an extension, you must write to us giving the reason that you need more time. We must receive your extension request in time to approve it before your current deadline or extension expires.

In the following example, the "if" clause was made into a separate sentence:

If you take less than your entitled share of production for any month, but you pay royalties on the full volume of your entitled share in accordance with the provisions of this section, you will owe no additional royalty for that lease of prior periods when you later take more than your entitled share to balance your account. This also applies when the other participants pay you money to balance your account.	Suppose that one month you pay royalties on your full share of production but take less than your entitled share. In this case, you may balance your account in one of the following ways without having to pay more royalty. You may either: (a) Take more than your entitled share in the future; or (b) Accept money from other participants.

Note that in the example above, the writer began the first sentences with "suppose that" and the second sentence with "in that case" to preserve the relationship between the two sentences.[4]

Sometimes we try to pile up ideas or verbs in a single sentence. This confuses the reader. Try to include only one or two ideas in each sentence. Padraic Spence gives the following example of a long sentence and its revision. The six verbs appear in boldface.

We **recommend** the Systems Development Division **prepare** a machine-checking program for the Exhibit 550 as soon as possible since this program **can save** time for the division, and because it **will advance** the dates by which finished output reports **can be** available, we **should assign** the project priority over all other projects.	We **recommend** the System Development Division **prepare** a machine-checking program for the Exhibit 550 as soon as possible. This program **can save** time for the division and **advance** the dates by which finished output reports **can be** available. Therefore, we **should assign** the project priority over all other projects.[5]

Scrap Business English Relics

Many of the expressions below were once considered standard business English. Several are standard legal expressions. Today they sound stiff, stale, or pompous.

The times change, and business English changes with them. We're more relaxed in our ways of dressing and speaking and living our lives; we can relax more in our writing, too.

As National Labor Relations Board Chairman John C. Truesdale and General Counsel Leonard R. Page state:

> Although it can be gratifying to sprinkle into our legal writing a "theretofore" now and then, a "whereby" or two, and a "hereinafter," unfortunately there is a cost to writing in that style. Legalese gets in the way of effectively communicating with the public we serve because legal jargon and Latin phrases are harder to understand than plain language.[6]

The following list shows how to update some worn-out expressions. The left column contains old business writing standards that now sound out of place. The right column suggests alternatives. Many of the alternatives will both improve your style and prevent confusion.

aforementioned (questionnaire)	omit; or say "the questionnaire I mentioned earlier"
allow me to point out; permit me to point out	please note
are in receipt of	received
as per your request	regarding your request
at an early date	soon; by (exact date)
at this time; at this point in time; at the present time	now

at this writing; as of this writing	omit; when else could it be? or say "now"
avail yourself of the opportunity	omit; or say "find time to; get the chance"
at your earliest convenience	omit; or say "as soon as you can" or "by (specific date)"
be of service to you	serve you; help you
contents noted	omit
desirous of	wish to
during such time as	when, while
enclosed please find/attached please find	please see the copy I've enclosed; the enclosed copy shows
feel	use "think" or "believe," unless you're expressing an emotion
for your information	omit
I have before me your letter	omit
I remain	omit
in a hasty manner	hastily; quickly
in compliance with your request	as you requested
a check in the amount of	a check for (amount); a (amount) check
in the event that	if
in the near future	specify when
kindly	please
legal terms: hereto, herewith, hereby, hereinafter, said, etc.	express in a simpler way
please be advised that	note that (or omit)
please contact me if you have any further questions	don't say unless you really mean it
pursuant to your request; in reference to your request	refer to previous correspondence more directly
recent date	specify date

referenced letter	the letter; the letter of (specified date)
regret to inform you	sorry to tell you
relative to	about
same (as in "we have cashed same")	it; the check
subject employee	he; she
take the liberty of (telling you)	omit; or say, "we'd like to tell you"
take this opportunity to	omit; get to the subject
thanking you in advance	presumptuous; say, "if you will (action), I will appreciate it"
the writer(s)	I/we
the undersigned	I/we
this letter will acknowledge	omit; get to the point
trusting you will; trusting this is	omit; introduces doubt
under separate cover	in another envelope; in an express mail letter, etc.
we wish to state	we believe, we want to assure you

Relax the Rules of a Time Gone By

Some of what we've been taught to think of as rules of grammar are really matters of usage; that is, of what is considered acceptable in using our language. Here are some rules that have now been relaxed or done away with:

- Don't use contractions in business writing. Today, using words like "it's," "don't," we're," and "here's" is seen as acceptable, and even advisable. These words help us cut through formality and make our writing friendly in tone.

- Never start a sentence with "and" or "but." Today, accepted English usage recognizes that starting a sentence with one of these words may be highly effective, or quite weak. Writers are allowed to follow their instincts.

- Never end a sentence with a preposition. Current opinion says that this rule is one you don't have to rely on.

Avoid Cumbersome, Roundabout Phrases

Many writers think that using more words will give them a more elevated style or a style that is proper for business correspondence. They use phrases when a word will do; they use expressions that are roundabout rather than to the point. The result is writing that is officious, cumbersome, and often confusing—a chore to read.

> "Please be advised that, in the event of fire, employees should avail themselves of the opportunity to exit via . . . "

Some cumbersome expressions and suggested remedies follow.

a large percentage of	many
a total of $250	$250
be in possession of	have
be of the opinion that	believe, think
despite the fact that	though
due to the fact that	due to, since, because
during which time	while
endeavor to ascertain	try to find out
exhibits a tendency to	tends to
for a period of a month	for a month
for the purpose of	to, for
give consideration to	consider
have occasion to be	have reason to be
in a manner of speaking	in a way

in the majority of instances	often, usually
in the month of April	in April
in a number of cases	sometimes
in reference to	about
in the nature of	like, as
in the neighborhood of	about
in the field of economics	in economics
in view of the fact that	in view of, since
make an appearance	appear
not in a position	unable
on or before	by
on the occasion of	at, during
range all the way from	range from
subsequent to	after
there are many people who think that	many people think
until such time	when
we deem it advisable	we suggest
with a view to	to
with regard to	about
without further delay	now

Delete Redundancies

Redundant writing repeats itself; it says, unintentionally, the same thing twice. Redundancies often creep in when we feel compelled to pad our business writing with filler phrases, such as those shown in parentheses below:

"Bulletins will be issued monthly (in the future)."

"I have not finished the report (at the present time)."

"The facility can handle (in the range of) 500 to 800 trainees."

Sometimes redundancies emerge when, in trying to make things absolutely clear, we overdo it. It's all too easy to say:

"The parts are (exactly) identical."

"We had no (other) alternative."

Some common redundant expressions include:

NOUN FORMS	*VERB FORMS*	*ADJECTIVE AND OTHER FORMS*
(total) annihilation	appoint (to the position of)	adequate (enough)
(major) breakthrough		big (in size)
capitol (building)	ascend (up)	(entirely) complete
(fellow) colleague	attach (together)	contemporary (in time)
(final) completion	climb (up)	each (and every)
consensus (of opinion)	coalesce (together)	(all) finished
(mutual) cooperation	combine (together)	first (and foremost)
courthouse (building)	commute (back and forth)	(exact) identical
(general) custom		large (in stature)
doctorate (degree)	congregate (together)	never (at any time)
(complete) destruction	continue (on, still)	(more) preferable
(baffling) dilemma	continue (to remain)	same (identical)
(sudden) eruption	cooperate (jointly)	sufficient (enough)
(necessary) essential	cover (over)	(completely) unanimous
(passing) fad	depreciated (in value)	unless (and until)
(basic) fundamentals	descend (down)	whether (or not)
(opening) gambit	eliminate (entirely)	
(free) gift	follow (after)	
(past) history	gather (together)	
(present) incumbent	join (together)	
(new) innovation	may (possibly)	
lawyer (by occupation)	merge (together)	
(twelve o'clock) midnight	name (as, to the position of)	
(personal) opinion	penetrate (into)	

complete (monopoly)
(final) outcome
(fellow) partner
(advance) planning
(troublesome)
   predicament
(leading) protagonist
(original) prototype
(temporary) reprieve
(local) resident
(end) result

(continue to) persist
prejudge (in advance)
(pre) plan
recall (back)
recur (again)
revert (back)
skirt (around)
spell out (in detail)

Sometimes we are repetitious in a different way: We simply repeat the same word or phrase over and over in the sentence or paragraph. Spence presents this example in a letter from his draft board:

> A personal appearance before the appeal board may be requested if you are eligible to request an appeal to the appeal board. You may appeal to the appeal board without requesting a personal appearance before the appeal board, but if you wish to appear before the appeal board, you must specifically ask for the appearance in addition to requesting an appeal.[7]

Prefer Short, Familiar Words to Long, Pretentious Words

Overblown words distract readers. They may end up paying more attention to how you're saying it than to what you're saying. And they may lose interest, especially if they have to look up words they don't know. Some inflated words and their deflated equivalents follow.

activate	begin
accomplished	done
aggregate	total
ameliorate	improve

approximately	about
ascertain	find
assist	help
categorize	sort
communicate	write, tell
construct	make
demonstrate	show
discontinue	stop
encounter	meet
endeavor	try
examination	test
facilitate	ease, simplify
indicate	show
initial	first
initiate	begin
modification	change
promulgate	publish
procure	get, buy
reside	live
terminate	end, stop
utilize	use

TEST YOURSELF: FINDING A BETTER WAY TO SAY IT

Translate each of the following "gobbledygook" statements into relaxed, straightforward business English:

1. We are agreeable to your request for the film.

2. Enclosed please find a check in the amount of $19.95.

3. Allow me to point out the merits of our plan.

4. The aforementioned appendix is being forwarded under separate cover.

5. Matter discussed herein is of a confidential nature.

6. In the event that this response is tardy, the undersigned regrets any inconvenience caused you.

7. Please respond at your earliest convenience.

8. We are not in receipt of the proposal at the time of this writing.

Answers can be found in the Appendix, page 309.

TEST YOURSELF: DEFLATING WORDS

Replace each inflated word with a short word (or with two or three short words).

1. employment	1.
2. finalize	2.
3. interface	3.
4. malfunctioning	4.
5. prioritize	5.
6. subsequently	6.
7. utilize	7.
8. whosoever	8.
9. optimum	9.
10. cognizant	10.

Answers can be found in the Appendix, page 310.

TEST YOURSELF: DEFLATING SENTENCES

To deflate these sentences, you'll have to interpret them. Rewrite each sentence to clarify its meaning; express the thought in an entirely different way if you like. Cut any unnecessary words. Whenever you can replace long words with short ones, or unfamiliar words with familiar ones, do so.

1. You will accelerate your career growth and attain a sizably increased income as you maximize your optimal attributes.

2. We deem inoperable your methodology for eliminating injurious behavioral patterns.

3. The established procedural practices cannot be adequately reconciled with maximum utilization of our human resources.

4. Radioactivity is presently an excessively dangerous possibility.

5. Because a majority of the students were inadequately prepared, their answers exhibited numerous inaccuracies.

Answers can be found in the Appendix, page 310.

Make the Parts Parallel

Making the parts parallel means using the same grammatical construction and beginning with the same part of speech. Notice that, in the preceding sentence, we did not say, "Making the parts parallel means that you should use..." We said, Making... means using..." The concept is this: Ideas that look roughly alike in your mind should look roughly alike on the page. In grammar, this is called parallel construction.

The following familiar phrases illustrate the use of parallel construction:

"One if by land, two if by sea."

"Where there's a will, there's a way."

"Saw sub, sank same."

"Ask not what your country can do for you; ask what you can do for your country."

Even if you're uncertain of the grammar principles involved, you can usually detect nonparallel items by using your ear. Nonparallel passages sound awkward. Listen to the following statements:

Nonparallel	Parallel
I came and then, when I saw, I was able to conquer.	I came, I saw, I conquered.
The steel companies lost money because of high costs, foreign competition had increased, and they had inefficient processes.	The steel companies lost money because of high costs, increased foreign competition, and inefficient processes.
We supported government of the people, thinking it should be by people.	We supported government of the people, by the people, and for the people.

Examples of Non-parallel Construction

There are specific ways to diagnose problems with parallelism, or to match the parts. Some common problems are:

- Using the wrong part of speech.

  Unmatched: "He was uninformed (adjective) and a fool (noun)."

  Matched: "He was uninformed (adjective) and foolish (adjective)."

- Shifting from active to passive voice.

  Unmatched: "We visited one field office, and selected files were analyzed."

  Matched: "We visited one field office and analyzed selected files."

- Shifting person.

  Unmatched: "First, one should pull the files and, next, you should put them in numerical order." (third person, second person)

  Matched: "First, pull the files and, next, put them in numerical order." (second person, second person)

Presenting Lists in Parallel Form

Lists are much easier to read when the items they contain are parallel. In the list on the left, three of the items begin with adverbs (what, where, when, and where), two with gerunds (getting, eating), and one with a noun (passport). In the list on the right, each item begins with a noun.

Nonparallel	Parallel
• passport	• passport
• what to wear and pack	• advice on what to wear
• where to stay	• hotels
• getting around the city	• transportation
• when and where workshops meet	• schedule of workshops
• eating out	• restaurants

Reasons for Matching the Parts

Making the parts parallel is important because:

- It makes the passage shorter.

- It makes the passage clearer.

- It puts you, the writer, in a better light. If the parts of your statements are not matched, the reader may begin to doubt your attention to detail and even the logic of your thinking.

TEST YOURSELF: MAKING THE PARTS PARALLEL

A. Make the parts of this outline match.

   1. Planning and Preparing

      a. The importance of setting objectives

      b. Determine what is negotiable

      c. Recognizing vulnerabilities

   2. How to Formulate an Opening Position

   3. How an Effective Presentation is Made

      a. Good first impression

      b. Opening a channel of communications

   4. Reaching Agreement

   5. Agreement Implementation

B. Here is part of an outline for a presentation on the benefits of higher education. Tighten it by making the parts match.

- Higher earnings over one's working life

- You can see how current events relate to the past

- Acquiring specialized knowledge

- Familiarity with the cultural side of life

- To gain insight into the human experience

C. Rewrite the following sentences to make the parts match.

1. The report discussing problem solving accompanies the one that discusses the making of decisions.

2. The team spent a week in the field, and several offices were visited.

3. Their staff members are friendly and work with efficiency.

D. The following are headings for sections of a memorandum. Put them in parallel form to strengthen the picture they give of the memorandum's overall structure. Make each heading as brief as possible.

An Introduction

This Study's Methodology

What Are the Major Problems?

Some Other Problems We Discovered

> What We Recommend
>
> In Conclusion
>
> E. Tell someone, step by step, how to use the copying machine at your office. Write the instructions below. Be sure to express the steps in parallel form.
>
> *Answers can be found in the Appendix, page 311.*

Others Tips for Writing More Clearly

Some simple guidelines will also help you make your writing clear:

- *If you use an acronym (abbreviation) your readers may not know, spell it out the first time you use it.* For example, "Department of Labor (DOL) contractors. . . ." In general, use abbreviations only to refer to terms that are central to the document. For example, if a regulation is about the Comprehensive Environmental Response, Compensation, and Liability Act, you can refer to it as CERCLA. Do not abbreviate terms you use only once or a few times. Write them out each time.

- *Use the same term consistently to identify a specific thought or object.* For example, if you use the term "senior citizen" to refer to a group, continue to use this term throughout your document. Do not substitute another term, such as "the elderly," that will make your reader wonder if you are referring to the same group.[8]

- *Use the simplest tense you can.* Use the present tense to avoid the clutter of compound verbs. A document written in the present tense is more immediate and forceful and less complicated. The following examples, which appear in *Writing User-Friendly Documents,* illustrate the use of simple tenses.

These sections describe types of information that would satisfy the application requirements of Circular A-110 as it would apply to this grant program.	These sections tell you how to meet the requirements of Circular A-110 for this grant program.
Applicants who were Federal employees at the time that the injury was sustained should have filed a compensation request at that time. Failure to do so could have an effect on the degree to which the applicant can be covered under this part.	You may not be covered under this part if: (a) You were a Federal employee at the time of the injury; and (b) You did not file a report with us at that time.

- *Avoid jargon whenever possible.* Jargon is the specialized vocabulary and idioms shared by those in the same organization, profession, etc. If a scientific, technical, or legal term is the best word to describe what you mean, use it. If you think your reader may be unfamiliar with the term, define it the first time you use it.

"Appellate litigation (lawsuits brought before a court of appeals) is conducted by attorneys in the national headquarters."

TEST YOURSELF: USING JARGON

List words that are shoptalk around your office or in your profession. How would you define these words for general readers?

BEING PRECISE

Read the following paragraph:

> Participants in the seminar said the curriculum related to the major responsibilities involved in their employment. They indicated that they had obtained information that would enable them to perform their obligations. One participant noted that the seminar design provided for concentration on certain areas for a given length of time.

Hard to grasp? Read it again. Still not clear?

The paragraph is a model of *imprecision*. You cannot read it and get a clear picture of what happened at the seminar; all you can do is try to interpret its meaning.

Now read the following paragraph and compare it to the one you just read:

> Nearly 85% of participants in the project management seminar said the curriculum covered the major responsibilities in their positions, including project planning, scheduling, and control. They said they had learned about calculating cost and schedule variances that would enable them to deal with unexpected changes in their projects. One participant noted that the seminar design provided for three hours of concentration in critical path scheduling.

The second paragraph gives much more specific information and is more persuasive. Precise words that give solid evidence help you convince the reader.

Imprecise: "The Detroit program is the best."

Precise: "The end-of-year evaluation of all the programs showed that the Detroit program achieved the highest placement rates."

In some kinds of writing, precision is a must. Those who write regulations, procedures, specifications, or technical instructions must include considerable detail; they must spell out exactly what is or is not to be done, and they must describe exceptions and variations. They must say exactly what is meant:

Imprecise: "The company will obtain space."

Precise: "The company will buy or rent space."

Imprecise: "A long document."

Precise: "A 515-page document."

Imprecise: "This check must be performed frequently."

Precise: "This check must be performed on the first and third Mondays of each month."

The challenge in writing that requires much detail and great exactness is to be both precise and readable. Sometimes, you must make tradeoffs.

Identify Your Audience Precisely

When you are writing about requirements, use singular nouns and verbs to prevent confusion about whether a requirement applies to individual readers or to groups.

Imprecise: "Individuals and organizations wishing to apply must file applications with the appropriate offices in a timely manner."

Precise: "You must apply at least 30 days before you need the certification.

(a) If you are an individual, apply at the State office in the State where you reside.

(b) If you are an organization, apply at the State office in the State where your head-quarters is located."[9]

TEST YOURSELF: PAINTING A CLEAR PICTURE

Read the following statements.

Now read into them. Use your imagination.

Replace each statement with one that is specific. Make it interesting and informative. Write more than one sentence if you like.

1. The study related to energy.

2. The meeting was well attended.

3. I work hard.

4. Their time-management problem needs attention.

5. The idea got a good reception.

6. They are uptight about the project.

Answers can be found in the Appendix, page 313.

AVOIDING COMMON BARRIERS TO UNDERSTANDING

It's always a good idea to read over what you've written—out loud or to your mind's ear. Put yourself in the reader's place. How do you sound? Clear, forceful, and lively? Sure of yourself? Firm but friendly? Intelligent but not arrogant?

Also be aware of the words as they roll off your tongue. Is the flow smooth? Or do you stumble in places? Are there some almost unpronounceable patches? Does the rhythm tend to fall flat?

The following are suggestions for diagnosing and remedying some of the common barriers.

Watch Out for "Noun Sandwiches"

Sometimes, the rule about being concise must be broken. The following group of words would trip up most readers:

> "last year's human resources management program evaluation results"

The tight knot of thoughts ("noun sandwich") needs to be loosened by the addition of prepositions and articles to clarify relationships among the words:

> "the results of last year's evaluation of the human resources management program"

Place Words Carefully within Your Sentences

Keep subjects and objects close to their verbs. The following sentence is both long and poorly constructed:

> "The project leader, after hearing all the results of the annual evaluation and weighing the pros and cons of the evaluation team's recommendations, decided to make five major changes in the program."

By the time the readers get to the verb "decided," they may have forgotten that the subject is project leader. Try this:

> "After hearing all the results of the annual evaluation and weighing the pros and cons of the evaluation team's recommendations, the project leader decided to make five major changes in the program."

Better still, put the ideas into two short sentences.

> "The project leader heard the results of the annual evaluation and weighed the pros and cons of the evaluation team's recommendations. He then decided to make five major changes in the program."

In this example from *Writing User-Friendly Documents*, it is difficult in the original version (the left column) to figure out which words relate to the forest products, which relate to the tribe, and which relate to the payments:

Upon the request of an Indian tribe, the Secretary may provide that the purchaser of the forest products of such tribe, which are harvested under a timber sale contract, permit, or other harvest sale document, make advance deposits, or direct payments of the gross proceeds of such forest products, less any amounts segregated as forest management deductions pursuant to section 163.25, into accounts designated by such Indian tribe.

If you ask us, we will require purchasers of your forest products to deposit their payment into an account that you designate.

(a) You can instruct us to deposit advance payments as well as direct payments into the account.

(b) We will withhold from the deposit any forest management deductions under section 163.25.[10]

- Put conditionals such as "only" or "always" and other modifiers next to the words they modify.

  Ambiguous: "You are only required to provide the following."

  Clear: "You are required to provide only the following."

Avoid Ambiguous Phrasing

Avoid ambiguous phrasing that can confuse your reader. The following is an example of such a phrase. The reader may have to read the statement several times to figure out that it doesn't mean "If you really want to have a disability. . . ."

  Ambiguous: "If you are determined to have a disability, we will pay you the following:"

  Clear: "If we determine that you have a disability, we will pay you the following:"

Make Pronoun References Clear

Have you cleared up any questions about which words your pronouns stand for? (In grammatical terms: Have you cleared up any faulty references?)

  Ambiguous: "The agencies have a number of field offices. Most of the work is done in them."

  Clear: "The agencies have a number of field offices. Most of the work is done in these offices."

Correct Dangling Modifiers

Have you made sure there are no dangling modifiers to confuse (or amuse) the reader?

> Dangling: "Imagine how we felt when, breaking through the clouds, Honolulu came into view."

But Honolulu did not break through the clouds. The plane did.

> Clear: "Imagine how we felt when the plane broke through the clouds and Honolulu came into view."

> Dangling: "After waiting 10 minutes, the engineer told us the elevator was not working."

But the engineer did not wait 10 minutes. You did.

> Clear: "After we'd waited 10 minutes, the engineer told us the elevator was not working."

Use Words Correctly—Especially Those That Are Similar

When you're concentrating on getting your thoughts down, it's easy to write one word when you mean another. It's also easy to use words carelessly, letting them slip by even though you're not sure that they're correct in the context.

Many errors are made because we mistake words that look and sound alike:

- affect/effect

- dual/duel

- ingenious/ingenuous

- principle/principal.

These errors can be embarrassing—but at least readers often understand despite them, and give us credit for what we meant to say. Sometimes, however, the misuse of words can mislead or perplex:

> "The idea literally blew them away." (Really? Or did it figuratively blow them away?)

> "We will not stand for the prosecution (persecution?) of the handicapped."

CHECKING YOUR READABILITY

A document's readability is the level of difficulty at which it is written, and therefore the level of education required to understand it. Readability is based on:

- The average length of sentences

- The average number of syllables in a word.

Readability of Familiar Publications[11]

The Atlantic Monthly	
The Wall Street Journal	Grade 12 (difficult)
The New York Times	Grade 11
Los Angeles Times	Grade 10
Business Week	Grade 10
Time magazine	Grade 10
Reader' Digest	Grade 10
Boston Globe	Grade 8
U.S.A. Today	Grade 8
People magazine	Grade 7
	Grade 6 (easy)

A document with long sentences and many syllables is considered more difficult to read than one with shorter sentences and fewer syllables. A 9th-grade level writing is about the right level for most business documents. This level uses few long words and keeps sentences to about 15 words in length.

There are several ways to determine a document's readability, including computer programs, readability graphs, and "Fog" indexes. These instructions are taken from Robert Gunning's *The Technique of Clear Writing*[12]:

1. Find the average number of words per sentence. Use a sample of at least 100 words. Divide the total number of words by the number of sentences. This gives you average sentence length.

2. Count the number of words of three syllables or more per 100 words. Don't count (a) words that are capitalized; (b) combinations of short, easy words like bookkeeper; and (c) verbs that are made three syllables by adding "ed" or "es"—like "created" or "trespasses."

3. Add the two figures above and multiply by 0.4. This will give you the Fog index. It corresponds roughly with the number of years of schooling a person requires to read a passage with ease and understanding.

TEST YOURSELF: USING A FOG INDEX

Calculate and compare the Fog index of two writing samples—yours or someone else's.

1. Which sample was easier to read?

2. How could you improve either or both of the samples?

The essence of plain language is clarity. Documents written in plain language are much more likely to be read, understood, and heeded—in much less time. Plain language means:

- Using shorter sentences
- Scrapping business English relics, including legal expressions
- Avoiding cumbersome phrases
- Eliminating redundancies
- Making parts (words, phrases, and items in a list) parallel
- Minimizing and explaining acronyms and jargon
- Avoiding confusing words and phrases, such as "noun sandwiches," dangling modifiers, ambiguous phrasing, and unclear pronoun references
- Placing words carefully within your sentence
- Using words correctly, especially those that look or sound alike
- Using simple tenses
- Using terms consistently.

Although brevity usually is preferable in writing, you sometimes must use more words to convey a more precise meaning. Make sure your reader gets a clear, convincing picture of what you mean.

You can get an idea how readable your documents are by using a Fog index, which is based on both sentence and word length. Although these are not the only determiners of plain writing, they are important.

---

[1]Miller, Mark R. *The Editorial Eye*, Alexandria, VA: EEI Press, March 1999. "Is It Plain English Yet? Bureaucratese makes people read between the lines."

[2]Kimble, Joseph. "Writing for Dollars, Writing to Please." *The Scribes Journal of Legal Writing* (1996-1997), vol. 6.

[3]Ibid.

[4]Writing User-Friendly Documents."
1998

[5]Spence, Padraic. *Write Smart: The Complete Guide to Business Writing.* Stockbridge, MA: The Water Street Press, 1996. page 96.

[6]"NLRB Publishes Revised Style Manual as Its Official Guide for Writing Legal Documents." <www.plainlanguage.gov/hotstuff/nlrb.htm>

[7]Spence, Padraic. *Write Smart: The Complete Guide to Business Writing.* Stockbridge, MA: The Water Street Press, 1996. page 7. Used with permission.

[8]Writing User-Friendly Documents."
1998.

[9]"Writing User-Friendly Documents."
1998.

[10]"Writing User-Friendly Documents."
1998.

[11]Dumaine, Deborah. *Write to the Top: Writing for Corporate Success.* New York: Random House, 1989.

[12]Gunning, Robert. *The Technique of Clear Writing.* New York: McGraw-Hill, 1968.

CHAPTER 6

Adding Visual Impact to Your Writing

Jazzing Up Your Document

Bill was working on a report for his boss's presentation before a congressional subcommittee. He had carefully planned and organized the report, drafted the paragraphs with topic sentences, checked for the proper tone, used the active voice, and performed a substantive edit to make sure it was complete but not wordy. Still, something did not seem right.

"It's boring to look at," Bill decided. "I need to add more white space, more headings, and more graphics."

To add white space, Bill increased the margins on all sides, added space between sections of the report, and made bulleted or numbered lists wherever he could. He also added headings for the sections of the report.

Then he re-read the document and thought about where graphics would be useful. "I don't want to just throw them in for decoration," he thought. He decided to use a line graph to show the effect of budget cuts on his agency's Public Information Office. To illustrate how the Office budgeted its time, he designed a pie chart with slices showing the different Office functions. A flow chart showed the route of information from the agency to the public. When he was done, Bill stepped back and looked at his document again.

"That's much better," he thought. "Now someone might actually *want* to read it."

In writing government documents, you want your readers to get information, comply with requirements, and apply for benefits with the least amount of effort. To help your readers understand what you are writing, you need to create visually appealing documents.

The Plain Language Action Network offers the following advice for replacing the often dense and confusing appearance of traditional government documents:

> Replace blocks of text with headings, tables, and more white space. You will help your reader by making the main points readily apparent and grouping related items together. Use a clear and uncrowded presentation and your readers will be more likely to understand what you want to convey.[1]

In this chapter, we will discuss how you can use these ideas to make your documents more visually appealing.

PLAIN LANGUAGE GUIDELINES FOR VISUAL FORMATTING

You can use appealing visual format to draw your readers' attention to information they need to know. *Writing User-Friendly Documents* offers the following tips:[2]

Layout

Margins

- Provide margins of 1-1/2 inches on either side of your text.

- Use justified left, but ragged right text throughout.

Headings

- Use upper and lower case, not all caps

- Set in boldface

- Justify to the left margin

- Triple-space before headings and double-space after (19.2 points before, 8.4 points after)

Typography

Fonts

- Use a proportionally spaced typeface like this one— rather than one in which all the letters have the same space, as in this example of `Courier` font.

- Avoid small, sans serif typeface like this, which is difficult to read. Instead, select a larger serif font like this one.

- Don't mix fonts *within the text.*

Shading/Boxing

- Use shading and boxing only to accent graphs, charts, etc.

Bullets

- Use standard bullets. If you select others, such as diamonds or arrows, be consistent.

- Generally, don't use more than two types of bullets in a letter.

- Use bullets instead of numbers except when you are presenting a sequence.

Bold/Italics/Underlining

- Use **bold** or *italics* for emphasis.

- Use italics for parenthetical information, like citations of laws.

Before You Finish

- Take a long look at the appearance of the document for eye-appeal.

- Be sure the document is not visually confusing.

- Don't overuse layout and typographical devices.

- Check for odd shapes (like the "hourglass effect") that may have unintentionally been created as you composed the letter.

ENHANCING THE TEXT WITH GRAPHICS

When you have many facts, the best way to present them is often with a table, graph, chart, or illustration. When you are discussing a lot of data, one table or figure can be clearer and more memorable than five pages of text. These visual aids help readers who are visual thinkers as well as those who have time only to skim.

When using graphics:

- Each of your figures and tables should have a *purpose*. Don't throw them in just to spice up your report.

- Each graphic should convey only *one main point*. First decide what point you want to make. Then choose the type of figure that can best represent the data and convey that point.

- Keep graphics *simple*. Cluttered and confusing tables and figures can be overwhelming.

- *Label* your graphics so the reader can clearly and easily see what each column of a table, axis of a graph, and wedge of a pie chart describes.

- Review each graphic to make sure it can *stand alone*. The reader should be able to understand it completely, *even if she or he has not read the text*. (Remember how many times *you* have flipped through a report, reading only the headings, graphs, and charts.)

- Each graphic should have a *caption*. The caption should do more than tell the reader what the graphic shows, e.g., "Homicide Rates of Industrialized Nations, 1960-1990." The caption should also summarize the main point you want the graphic to convey—the bottom line or reason you included it in the first place. These captions may be written in sentence form, e.g., "Since 1960, the U.S. homicide rate has been more than ten times that of any other industrialized nation."

Although visual aids can enhance writing, they should only be used as a supplement for information discussed in the text. Make sure that you refer to the visual aid in the text, using the following guidelines:

- Try to place a visual aid on the same page as, or on the page next to, the text in which it is discussed.

- Refer to its location in the text. For example, "The following table. . . ." or "On the opposite page is. . . ."

- If you decide to put your visual aid in a separate section, such as an appendix, note its location in the text.

TYPES OF VISUAL AIDS

The following table illustrates some common types of visual aids and their uses.

Type of Visual	What It Shows	How to Use It
photograph	An exact image of the item's appearance	to show an item exactly as it looks
line drawing	An artist's rendering of what something looks like	to show shape or detail, but also information about process or operation (for example, arrows to indicate direction)
cutaway diagram	The inside of an item, relative to the exterior	to show the insides of mechanisms, buildings, and structures
exploded diagram	The different physical elements of a mechanism and the way they fit together	to show how to assemble or disassemble a mechanism
map	An item's location relative to other items	to show an item's position and distance from other items, in order to help the reader locate the item.
flow chart	Stages of a process	to show the steps in a process and to the operator through alternatives
schematic	Stages of a process and the layout of parts in that process	to show the steps in a process, and the physical layout of each step

Type of Visual	What It Shows	How to Use It
table	a large body of data	to show large amounts of detailed information; to display exact numbers; and to compare individual entries and categories
line graph	The way one variable changes in relation to another	to show trends over time and to compare trends
pie chart	Proportions and percentages	to show relative amounts of various segments of a whole population
bar chart	Comparisons among quantities	to compare various items for a particular time or to show how one item changes over time

The following are some examples of visual aids and tips for their use.

Using Photographs Effectively

Use photographs to:

- Record an event

- Show the shape and surface appearance of an object

- Illustrate the development of a phenomenon over a period of time

- Show objects that are difficult to draw

- Show actual appearances where details, color, tones, and textures are important

- Prove something is real.

To make the use of photographs effective:

- Remove any distracting details by zooming in or cropping the photograph.

- Draw attention to the subject through focus, angle, and lighting.

- Place a familiar object, such as a ruler, book, or person, near the object being photographed (to show relative size).

- Show depth through use of lighting and focus.

Do not use a photograph to show a process where flow is involved.

Photograph

Using Drawings Effectively

Use drawings to:

- Show the appearance of an object or scene without unnecessary detail

- Show views impossible to create through photography without destroying the subject in the process

- Show objects that do not exist yet

- Emphasize the significant part of a mechanism or its function

- Focus on relationships or details that a photograph cannot capture.

To make the use of drawings effective:

- Omit any details in the drawing that do not contribute to the point you are trying to make.

- Emphasize parts of the drawing that carry the most information, such as the outline.

- Show equipment and other objects from the point of view of the person who will use them.

- Draw different parts of a drawing in proportion to one another, unless you indicate that certain parts are enlarged.

- Place labels where necessary for comprehension.

- Select the type of drawing to match the audience, such as:

  —cutaways for general audience;

  —exploded views for mechanics; and

  —cross-sections for engineers.

The following are examples of how drawings can be used as visual aids:

Line Drawing

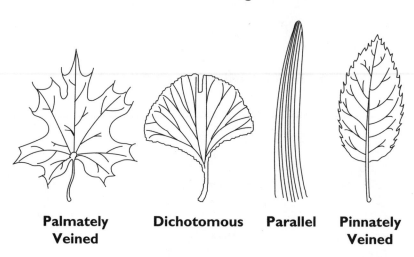

| Palmately Veined | Dichotomous | Parallel | Pinnately Veined |

Cutaway Diagram

Exploded Diagram

 Hose Clamp

 Hose

 Hose Clamp

 Nipple

 Washer

Lid

Nut

 Foam container

Using Maps Effectively

Use maps to show:

- Where things are located in relation to each other and to the reader's current location

- Geographical distribution of data or objects

- A complicated system or terrain.

To make the use of maps effective:

- Keep maps simple; display only necessary details.

- Use obvious or familiar symbols.

- Follow natural color conventions (e.g., using blue for water).

- Simplify the display when possible without distorting crucial relationships.

- Include a display and a full legend.

Map

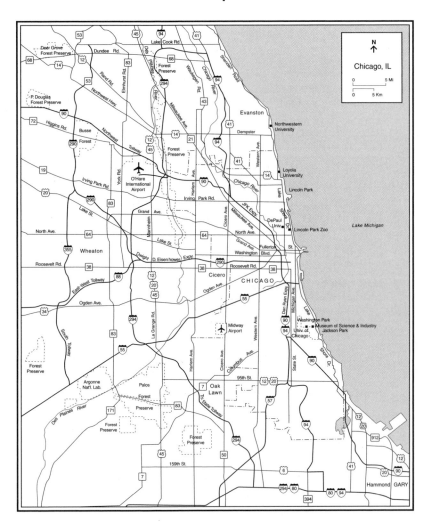

Using Flow Charts Effectively

Use flow charts to show:

- Stages in a process

- Sequence of steps in a procedure from beginning to end

- Interrelationships among the stages in a process.

Flow charts are diagrams that show the stages in a process, indicating the sequence in which the stages occur. Flow charts consist of arrows to indicate flow and icons to represent each stage in the process. Icons might include:

- Labeled blocks

- Pictorial representations

- Standardized symbols

    —circles or oblongs to indicate starts and stops;

    —squares or rectangles to indicate actions;

    —diamonds to indicate stages at which the performer must make a decision; and

    —hexagons to indicate stages at which the performer must make a check.

When using flow charts:

- Make flow from left to right or top to bottom.

- Label each stage.

- Include a key for symbols your readers may not understand.

Flow Chart

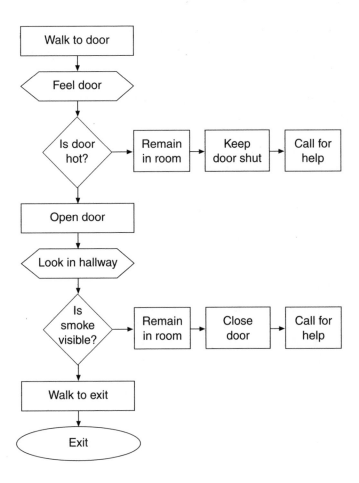

Using Schematics Effectively

Schematic diagrams are used primarily in electronics, chemistry, and electrical and mechanical engineering. Use them to:

- Show an operation with lines and symbols rather than physical likeness

- Emphasize the relationships among the parts at the expense of precise proportions.

To make the use of schematics effective:

- Make clear in the text why the schematic is included.

- Include only necessary information.

- Keep terminology and abbreviations consistent.

- Position labels horizontally for ease of reading, if possible.

- Consider your reader's ability to understand the symbols in your schematic. (Symbols and their meanings are like a foreign language.)

Schematic

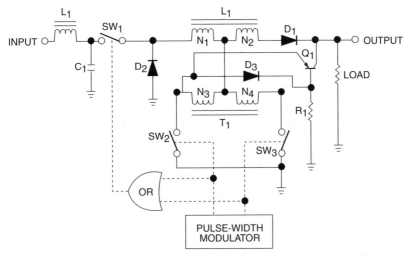

Modulated voltage regulator

Using Tables, Line Graphs, Pie Charts, and Bar Charts Effectively

To show how the same information can be presented in different ways, let's take a look at a summary of some data from the Bureau of Labor Statistics:

> Over the 1998-2008 period, the percentage of jobs in the service-producing industries is expected to increase in comparison with the percentage of jobs in the goods-producing industries. In 1988, service-producing industries made up 66.2% of the jobs. In 1998, service-producing industries made up 70.8% of the jobs; in 2008, they are expected to make up 73%. In 1988, goods-producing jobs made up 20.9% of the jobs. In 1998, good-producing industries made up 18% of the jobs; in 2008, they are expected to make up 16%.[3]

While this summary reports the necessary information, it would make for a very dry presentation. How about showing your audience what you are talking about? One way to do that is with a table.

Table

Employment by Major Industry Division, 1988, 1998, and Projected 2008[4]

	Distribution by Percent 1988	Distribution by Percent 1998	Distribution by Percent 2008
Goods-Producing	20.9	18.0	16.0
Service-Producing	66.2	70.8	73.0
Other	12.9	11.2	11
Total	100	100	100

Use tables to:

- Present a large amount of detailed information in a small space

- Facilitate detailed, item-to-item comparisons

- Show numerous facts precisely.

To make the use of tables effective:

- Design the table for quick scanning.

- Make the table complete, so that the reader does not need to refer to surrounding text. Give each table a title and column heads.

- Keep information within the table consistent. For example, include the same number of decimal points for all numbers in a column.

While the table presents information in a convenient form, it does not enable the reader to see the data. To do that, use line graphs, bar charts, or pie charts.

Line Graph

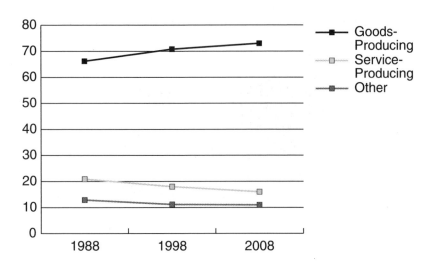

Now you have a better idea of what the changes in distribution of jobs looks like. Another way to see this change is through a pie chart. However, the pie chart can only show us one year at a time.

Pie Chart

Employment by Major Industry Division, 1988

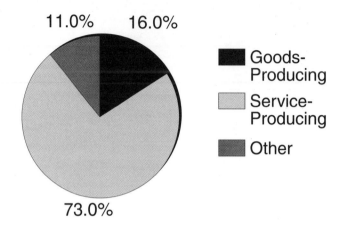

To see all three years depicted, we need a bar chart:

Bar Chart

Employment by Major Industry Division, 1988, 1998, and Projected 2008

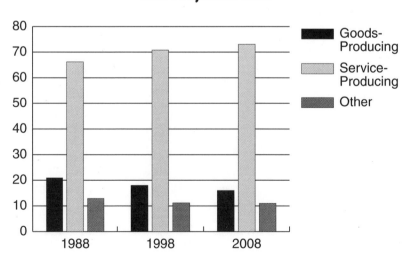

Bar charts can either compare various items for a particular time (e.g., Population of the Six Major Regions of the U.S., 1900) or show how one item changed over time (e.g., Population of the Middle Atlantic States, 1800-1950). Bar charts can have single or multiple bars. Hints:

- Label both the horizontal and vertical axes.

- Make sure all the bars are the same width. The space between the bars should be about one-half the width of the bars.

As you can see, we use specific charts and graphs for specific purposes. It's useful to know when and how to use each graphic most effectively.

Use graphs, pie charts, and bar charts to:

- Emphasize trends, relationships, and patterns in the data

- Forecast and predict future trends

- Present large amounts of complex data

- Add credibility

- Induce the reader to read the text.

To make their use effective:

- Keep charts simple.

- Focus on the data, displaying it so trends stand out.

- Avoid misleading charts.

- Graduate the vertical and horizontal scales so that they give an accurate visual impression of the data. To prevent distortion, keep the scales in constant ratio with each other.

- Include all titles, notes, and annotations needed to make the chart clear and complete.

- Use similar symbols, textures, or colors for related items of data.

- Use different symbols, textures, or colors to distinguish separate data elements or series.

- Use curves and lines to show trends and to connect data points.

- Include a key to list and explain symbols when necessary.

To help your readers understand the information they need, you need to create visually appealing documents. This means using white space, short sections, easy-to-read type, frequent headings, and bulleted and numbered lists, as well as bold-face and italics for emphasis.

Graphics also add visual appeal and can aid a reader's comprehension of a document. The following are some common types of visual aids that you can use to enhance your writing and supplement information:

- Photographs
- Line drawings
- Cutaway diagrams
- Exploded diagrams
- Maps
- Flow charts
- Schematics
- Tables

- Line graphs
- Pie charts
- Bar charts.

All graphics should be labeled clearly, have a caption, and make sense—even if the reader does not read the text.

---

[1]*Writing User-Friendly Documents.* <www.plainlanguage.gov>

[2]"Guidelines for Using Layout and Typography to Create Effective Emphasis." <www.plainlanguage.gov/howto/appears.htm>

[3]Bureau of Labor Statistics. "BLS Releases New 1998-2008 Employment Projections." Nov. 30, 1999. <stats.bls.gov/emphonme.htm>

[4]Ibid. "Table 1: Employment by Major Industry Division, 1988, 1998, and Projected 2008."

CHAPTER 7

Editing: The Final Phase

One Step at a Time

Jane's boss, Lee, asked her to edit the manuscript of the new consumer protection handbook. After a few days, Jane handed it back in.

"Great job, Jane," Lee said. "Tell me, how did you manage to do that so quickly and accurately?"

"I did it in several stages," Jane said. "The first day or so, I looked at the document in its entirety—the 'big picture.' I checked to see that it was well organized, complete, and logical. I made sure the main idea of each section and each paragraph was clear. Next, I copyedited, looking first at the sentences, checking for active voice, subject-verb agreement, and all that. Finally, I checked the spelling, punctuation, and capitalization. When I was done, I had Frank and Anne each review it. They found some things I had missed."

"Yes, it's always good to have more than one set of eyes looking at a document," Lee said.

"And one other important thing," Jane said. "I found that I needed to put it down occasionally and take a break. When I came back, I was able to look at it with fresh eyes."

"Well, keep those eyes fresh," Lee said. "I'll need you to proofread the handbook when it comes back from the printer."

People are often tempted to ignore the final editing phase, but doing so is risky. A thoughtful editorial review is the last line of defense for every document. It's a shame that "editors are so often told, 'Do only a light copyedit, there's not time or money for more,'" says Jane Rea, manager of editorial services for EEI Communications. "You can't skimp on the editing step and still hope to get a readable product."[1]

It is important to review your work to make sure that your writing achieves its purpose; your ideas are stated clearly and correctly; and your writing is free of spelling, grammatical, and other mechanical errors. Remember, even professional writers rely on editors to cast a critical eye on their work.

TWO TYPES OF EDITING

When we discuss editing, we are really referring to two different types of critical review: substantive editing and line (or copy) editing. In *substantive* editing, you review the overall development of the writing, looking at how well the ideas are organized and developed and how well they are presented. In *line editing*, you check subject-verb agreement, verb tense, active and passive voice, understandability, precision, and readability, as well as the mechanics of writing, such as spelling and punctuation.

Substantive Editing

During this step, look at the overall picture. Ask yourself, "Did I follow my outline? Did I include the ideas I wanted to include? Did I develop those ideas properly? Did I present them in a logical order? Did I present those ideas in a way that makes them understandable?" *In other words, "Did I say what I wanted to say?"*

Consider what you've said, and put yourself in the reader's place. Read only what you've put on the page; don't read in what you know but have left unsaid. If possible, have someone who is totally unfamiliar with the subject read it.

The following checklist can help you make sure that your writing is doing what you want it to do:

- *Did I state my purpose?* Do my ideas and the organization of them help me achieve that purpose?

- *Did I say enough?* Did I follow my outline and make all the points I intended to make?

- *Did I say too much?* Did I digress from my outline? If so, is the departure justified? Have I repeated myself?

- *Did I consider my audience?* Is what I have written understandable and useful to the people who will be reading it? Did I say enough to inform them, without saying too much?

- *Did I put the "bottom line on top"* (the main idea first)?

- *For each section, did I put the main idea first?*

- *Does each idea have its own space?* Are ideas presented clearly and logically, with no ideas hidden or thrown in at the end without being fully developed?

- *Did I make good use of white space?* White space between paragraphs makes each paragraph stand out visually. Indents or bullets help show how ideas are subordinate to each other. In this checklist, for example, bullets show that each item is part of the main checklist.

- *Did I use headlines and sub-headlines* to help the reader understand my organization?

- *Are my conclusions developed?* Are they understandable? Did I say enough to support them? Did I say too much?

- *Have I used transitional words* to help the reader see the connections between my ideas?

Line Editing (Copy Editing)

Once you have looked at the overall picture, it is time to check the smaller details, like the development of paragraphs and sentences. Now is the time to think about word choice, tone, style, readability, understandability, and precision. As you read over something, think about how it sounds to you.

Line editing also means checking for proper and consistent spelling, punctuation, capitalization, abbreviation, word division, and the like—matters that are sometimes referred to as the *mechanics* of writing. The purpose of line editing is to eliminate any errors or inconsistencies as well as any awkward features that might distract the reader from what is being said.

The following checklist can help you with line editing:

- Check the *paragraphs*. Does each paragraph have unity (that is, does it cover one main idea)? Does it have a topic sentence that introduces that main idea?

- Check the *sentences*. Does each sentence cover one idea? If a sentence covers more than one idea, should it be broken into two sentences? Are the sentences varied in structure?

- Check the *verbs*. Do you use the active voice, in which the subject of the sentence is performing the action, whenever possible?

- Check for *submerged verbs*. Are there any verbs that have been submerged under helping verbs and turned into nouns (such as, "He made an assessment" instead of "He assessed")?

- Check your *choice of words*. Did you use plain English? Or did you find yourself using:

—bureaucratese ("At this point in time, we estimate that implementing this program will impact..." instead of "We now believe this program will affect...")

—cliches ("six of one and half a dozen of another")

—gobbledygook ("electronically adjusted, color-coded vehicular-flow control mechanism" instead of "traffic light")

—coined words ("ultra-self-orientationability" instead of "ability to orient itself").

- Do your words convey the appropriate *tone*—the right amount of friendliness and directness? Or do you sound overly familiar, arrogant, or unsure?

- Do you use *gender-neutral language*? Do you avoid using "he" when referring to either male or female? Do you refer to a "stewardess" or a "flight attendant"? A "policeman" or "police officer"? "Mankind" or "humanity" (or "humankind")?

- Are you *understandable*? Do you choose simple, direct phrases and familiar words? Or do you rely on stiff, pompous-sounding expressions? Do you use too many acronyms?

- Are you *precise*? Do you use vague terms ("large") or specific words that clearly state what you mean ("nine inches")?

- Are you *too wordy*? Instead of telling the reader the time, are you telling him how to build a clock?

- Have you *punctuated correctly*? Have you used:

—commas as slow-down signs?

—semicolons as stop-and-go-again signs?

—colons as stop-and-look-what's-next signs?

—periods as full-stop signs?

PROOFREADING

Your work as a business writer is not truly done until you have seen your manuscript through to the end. You need to *proofread* to make sure that the finished product reflects the care you put into planning, writing, and revising. Although the term "proofreading" originally meant the reading of printers' proofs to detect errors, it now refers to the checking of any final product. You need to double-check for any details that may have slipped by you as you pored over your computer screen. It's a good idea to see your manuscript in hard copy to help you spot difficulties.

Sheryl Lindsell-Roberts says this about proofreading:

> *Proofreading* is akin to quality control. In a manufacturing environment, quality control is making sure the merchandise is free from defects so the customer doesn't wind up with a lemon. In the world of writing, it means making sure that the document is free from errors so it reflects well on you, the writer.[2]

Ask yourself:

• Does the "rule of 10" apply? That is, are all numbers of two or more digits presented as figures, while all one-digit numbers are presented as words? (Check your style manual.)

- Am I correct in capitalizing Eastern Standard Time?

- Should I insert a comma after the last element of a series—for example: thinking, writing, and editing. (Again, check your style manual.)

- When I wrote Tuesday, March 20, did I check to make certain March 20 is a Tuesday?

- Did I double-check the spelling of all names of people, titles, and organizations?

- Did I double-check all numbers?

- Did I write *principle* instead of *principal*, or *it's* instead of *its*?

HOW DOES A STYLE MANUAL HELP?

A style manual provides guidelines for correctness and consistency regarding the mechanics of language. You are likely to have questions that are not answered in these style manuals. Sometimes a good dictionary will help. At other times, you will have to rely on your preference and judgment. Whatever alternative you choose, use it consistently.

The following are among the most widely used style manuals:

- *The Associated Press Stylebook and Libel Manual* (Reading, Mass., Addison-Wesley Publishing Company, 1992). Used by journalists and editors, this stylebook is organized like a dictionary. It contains useful appendices on copyright guidelines, the Freedom of Information Act, photo captions, and proofreaders' marks.

- *The Chicago Manual of Style*, 14th Edition (Chicago, The University of Chicago Press, 1993). Many writers in academia and business consider this the standard style guide. It has many useful sections, including ones on punctuation, quotations, and abbreviations.

- *The United States Government Printing Office Style Manual* (Washington, U.S. Government Printing Office, 1984). This is the authority for writers, editors, typists, typesetters, and printers throughout the government. The manual covers matters from capitalization to plant and insect names, and even has sections on foreign languages. It contains a helpful list of standard proofreading marks.

More specific style manuals are published by the following organizations:

- American Chemical Society

- American Mathematical Society

- American Psychological Association

- Council of Biology Editors

- International Steering Committee of Medical Editors

- Modern Language Association

- United States Geological Survey.

Different style manuals may list different rules for printing the same information, depending in part on the needs of those who regularly use the manual. For a better understanding of how style manuals differ, consider the following chart:

Comparing Style Manuals

Style Guide	Abbreviations for state names in conjunction with cities	Capitalization of professional titles	Dates	Foreign words and phrases	Numbers	Decades
AP	Use abbreviations provided ("Birmingham, Ala.")	Capitalize only directly before a name ("Secretary of Defense William Perry")	"Oct. 18, 2001"	Do not italicize; place in quotation marks and explain if unfamiliar	Spell out whole numbers below 10	"the 1990s"
Chicago	Spell out except in tables, lists, reference materials, and addresses	Capitalize only directly before a name ("Secretary of Defense William Perry")	"18 October 2001"	italicize if likely to be unfamiliar	Spell out whole numbers below 100	"the 1990s"
GPO	Use Postal Service abbreviations ("Birmingham, AL")	In specified instances, capitalize after a name ("William Perry, Secretary of Defense")	"October 18, 2001" (or, in the military, "18 October 2001")	do not italicize unless specifically requested	Spell out whole numbers below 10	"the 1990's"

TIPS ON COPY EDITING AND PROOFREADING

The approach outlined below is designed especially for checking long documents. But you can develop your copy editing and proofreading skills by practicing the approach with shorter documents.

1. Find a quiet place and force yourself to concentrate. *Tackle the job systematically.* Don't try to see too many things at once.

2. To begin, focus on groups of words in sentences and paragraphs.

    a. The first time through, read only for *meaning.*

        — Does what is there, on the page, make sense?

        — Has anything been left out?

        — Are all references and citations accurate?

    b. Next time, check the *mechanics.*

        — Are the sentences grammatically correct?

        — Is the punctuation correct?

3. Now try to focus on *individual words.* (It helps to read backwards, starting with the last word and working back to the first).

    a. Are there any typos?

    b. Are the words spelled correctly?

    c. Are the words capitalized correctly and consistently?

    d. Are the words abbreviated correctly and consistently?

    e. Are the words divided correctly and consistently?

    f. Are figures and symbols used correctly and consistently?

4. Now look at the document *as a whole.*

    a. Are the parts arranged appropriately and evenly on the page?

       — Are the margins adequate?

       — Does the white space reflect the thought structure?

       — Are the indentations consistent?

       — Is the spacing consistent?

    b. If there is more than one page:

       — Does each page have a number?

       — Are the pages in order?

    c. If there is more than one part:

       — Are all the parts (attachments, enclosures, appendices, table of contents, bibliography, exhibits, etc.) included and in order?

       — Is each part labeled correctly and clearly?

       — Are titles and headings typed consistently?

Frequently Used Proofreader's Marks

⊙ Insert period

: Insert colon

? Insert question mark

=/ Insert hyphen

❝❞ Insert quotation marks

⊥ Insert 1-en dash
N

⊏/⊐ Insert brackets

Insert space

⌇ Delete

Stet Let it stand—used in
margin

ᶴᶜ Small caps—used in
margin

Caps All caps—used in
margin

ℓc Lowercase—used in
margin

¶ Paragraph

⊐ Move right

⌐ Move up

⊐⊏ Center horizontally

⌄ Insert comma

; Insert semicolon

! Insert exclamation point

⌄ Insert apostrophe

⊥ Insert 1-em dash
M

(/) Insert parentheses

◌ Close up

◌ Delete and close up

•••••• Let it stand—used
in text under affected
letters

══ Small caps—used in text
under affected letters

≡ All caps—used in text

/ Lowercase—used in text on
affected letters

No ¶ No paragraph

⊏ Move left

⊔ Move down

⊔⊓ Center vertically

‖	Align vertically	=	Align horizontally
tr	Transpose—used in margin	↶	Transpose—used in text around affected letters
ital	Italic—used in margin	—	Italic—used in text under affected letters
bf	Boldface—used in margin	∿∿	Boldface—used in text under affected letters
/	Used in text to show deletion or substitution	∧	Caret—indicator used to mark position of change

EDITING SOMEONE ELSE'S DOCUMENT

Editing someone else's writing requires objectivity, maturity, and tact. A writer has put time and effort into creating a document, and is putting his or her ego on the line when giving it up for editing. Therefore, as an editor, try to be balanced, specific, constructive, and gentle.

Read the draft once in its entirety before making any marks on it. Then ask yourself the questions for substantive editing. When you read your draft through again, consider the points related to line editing.

Only after you have carefully considered your comments should you begin writing—with a pencil, not a pen, so that you can change your comments if necessary. Guidelines for editing someone else's work include:

- Make no change unless you can give a good reason for it.

- Focus on the document and its impact on the intended reader, not on your preferences.

- Use good judgment in responding to what has been written. If a piece of writing is good, return it with a note saying, "Nice work" or "Great job."

- If the document needs substantial editing, take the time to talk to the writer. Suggest some changes you feel are necessary and explain why. Provide gentle instruction as needed, not scolding.

- Remember that your job as an editor is to look at a document objectively—something that is impossible for a writer to do.

FIELD TESTING YOUR WRITING

It is important to get feedback from people who are likely to use your document. We often write documents that are more suitable for ourselves than for our readers. Make sure that you test what you write. Always have someone else read and comment on what you write.

If you are preparing documents that will be widely circulated, conduct a field test among people who represent your audience. This process will tell you if your audience *wants to read* your work, *can read* it, and *can make use* of it. The Plain Language Action Network describes three methods of testing: focus groups, protocol testing, and control studies.[3]

Focus Groups

A focus group is run with a small group (usually 8-12) people. The moderator prepares a list of questions or a script in advance and may use a one-way mirror for observers or a tape recorder to help ensure an accurate report. The moderator should ask questions that generate discussion and that will not bias the answers.

Although focus groups may give some qualitative (What do people think about it?) information, they are not usually an effective way to test the usability of a letter or to learn how well an individual really understands what you have written.

Protocol Testing

Protocol testing is a qualitative technique that tests the usability of a document. This one-on-one interview technique with the reader is extremely valuable in determining if the reader is interpreting your message the way you intended. Here are the steps:

1. Ask the reader to read to a specific cue, usually a dot indicating a stopping point.

2. Each time the reader reaches the cue, ask for an explanation of what that section means.

3. At the end of the document, ask additional questions, such as:

   —What would you do if you got this document?

   —Do you think the writer was trying to help you?

4. For longer documents, test the document as a whole, not just individual paragraphs. Note how often the reader has to flip from page to page to find references, for example.

5. Conduct six to nine interviews on each document.

The following is an example of how protocol testing uncovered misunderstanding on the part of readers.

The Veterans Benefits Administration (VBA) tested a letter in which readers appeared to understand every word. However, when asked what they would do if they got this letter, most people said they would call VBA's toll-free number. The letter was about a replacement check sent because the original check was now out of date. The letter said, "You will receive the new check shortly." Readers indicated that they would call if they didn't receive the check the same time as the letter. Changing the sentence to show an approximate date they would receive the check eliminated countless phone calls.

In another situation, some readers were confused by the VA term "service-connected disability." To VBA, it means that a veteran has a disability that can be traced back to his/her time in military service. Protocol tests showed that one veteran thought it meant a disability that happened at work. Another veteran was injured while in the military, but not while on duty, and did not know if he had a service-connected disability.

When each reader was asked a general question about understanding the letter, they all said that it was clear. Yet several would have done something different than what VBA wanted because they assumed a different definition of "service-connected." The solution was to explain the phrase so that everyone was working from the same definition.

Control Studies

Control studies allow you to collect quantitative data on how well the general public uses the final document you've produced. To conduct a control study, follow these steps:

1. Before you conduct the study, think about what would make your document successful—what kind of results you want. For example:

    — Do you want *more calls* regarding a certain program?

— Do you want *fewer calls* asking for clarification?

— Do you want *more people* to return an application or payment?

— Are there certain parts of the application that you would like to be completed *more accurately*?

2. Send a small group of people the new version of your document.

3. Send the same number of people the old version.

4. Ask members of both groups to respond to your document, preferably in writing.

5. Track the responses of both groups.

6. Record responses. (For example, you can record what percentage of your "before document" generates correct responses compared to your "after documents.")

It's a good idea to use control studies after your qualitative testing is completed and you believe you have the best possible document. This is because control testing will tell you *if* the new document is a success, but it won't tell you *why* it is or isn't a success.

When to Use What Tool

Focus groups and control groups are optional, depending on what type of document you are rewriting. However, protocol testing is an essential tool to help you determine where to make changes in your document. The following chart shows the most effective times to use each tool:[4]

Three Methods of Field Testing

Method of Testing	When to Use It	What You Will Get
Protocol Test (qualitative)	After completing a final draft of your document	• Specific information about what readers think your document means. • Information about what readers will do with the document when they receive it. • Observations about how they read your document and how well they can follow the format. This should be the basis of any revisions needed to the document.
Focus Groups (qualitative)	• Before rewriting an old, usually lengthy, document • After rewriting to compare the format of different versions of a document	• Information about how readers feel about the old document—what they like and don't like. • What information they need that they don't have. This can be a basis for how you rewrite the new document. When focus groups are used to decide on format, the content should already be protocol-tested. The content should be the same for each version.
Control Group (quantitative)	After protocol testing and revising a document	• Data about how many people did what you wanted. • A comparison between the old document and the new document This information can help determine the success of the rewrite.

Joseph Kimble is a strong advocate of document testing:

> . . . we do need to give more attention to testing major documents, and not just legal documents. Government and businesses send out forms, notices, brochures, and bills by the thousands and hundreds of thousands. Testing a draft costs money. But even some testing is better than none; some kinds of testing are not expensive; and whatever testing is done on mass documents should pay for itself many times over.[5]

TEST YOURSELF: LINE EDITING A LETTER

Suppose the letter below were going out over your signature. What changes would you make before it is mailed? Examine the letter for things that look or sound strange. Look out for inconsistencies, omissions, errors, problems with tone and style, submerged verbs, and parts that are not parallel. Is the letter understandable? Is the phrasing precise? Circle each mistake you notice and rewrite the letter.

See the Appendix, page 314, for an example of how to revise the letter.

Dear Mrs. Jones;

Thank you for inquiring about changes planned for this year's Youth Leadership Institute (Y.L.I.) program.

Lessons learned from last year
Many participants said that last year's YLI program was the best of its kind. However, the program showed the need to provide 24-hour direction to the program participants. Therefor, Behavioral Sciences has made a suggestion that this year's instructors undergo new screening procedures. This screening would identify whether instructors have the background in psychology needed for

---

providing 24-hr. monitoring of students; crisis counseling abilities; and screening for substance abuse problems.

Last year's student progress evaluation program survey results showed that, despite attempts to compensate for false results caused by students' unwillingness to discuss their concerns, the evaluation program too often did not reflect students' progress accurately.

Changes planned for this year

To address the survey problem, we are developing a new survey system which uses both instructor-led interviews and anonymous questionnaires. Both surveys will be administered frequently. Students will participate in both programs, and instructors will use the anonymous questionnaire results to gauge the overall progress of the students as a body. We hope to optimize this year's survey findings with this new system.

We are also preparing to implement the suggested instructor screening program, with input from Behavioral Sciences and from the Personnel Department.

In view of the fact that we are making these changes, we will send you copies of all pertinent forms and questionnaires when they become available. Please call if you need more info.

Sincerely,

Reviewing your documents is absolutely essential. After spending hours or days preparing a letter or report that you're proud of, you don't want to send it out with even one error because, unfortunately, the error is what your reader remembers.

Reviewing documents includes three steps: substantive editing, line editing, and proofreading. In some cases, you may add an important fourth step: testing.

In *substantive editing,* you look at the "big picture"—the overall development of your writing. At this stage, you read over your document to make sure it is logical, understandable, complete, well organized, and directed toward the audience.

Next, you *line edit* your document. Now is the time to check the smaller details, like development of paragraphs and sentences, usage and spelling of words, and punctuation.

When you have what you believe is your final copy, it's important to double-check for any details that may have slipped by you. Be especially careful to re-check the spelling of all names of people, titles, and organizations; numbers; dates; word usage; capitalization; and punctuation.

A style manual is invaluable during the copy editing and proofreading stages of the writing process. Make sure you are aware of differences among style manuals and that you follow the one used by your office. Use the United States Government Printing Office Style Manual if you are a federal employee.

When you edit someone else's work, try to be balanced, specific, constructive, and gentle. Your job is to look at a document objectively—something that is impossible for a writer to do.

After you have edited and proofread your document, always have someone else read and comment on what you wrote. If you are preparing documents that will be widely circulated, conduct a field test among people who represent your audience. Three methods of testing are focus groups, protocol testing, and control studies. Focus groups and protocol testing yield qualitative information, while control studies give you quantitative data. All three are useful in specific situations; protocol testing is essential after you have completed the final version of your letter or report.

[1]Miller, Mark R. "Is It Plain English Yet? Bureaucratese Makes People Read Between the Lines" *The Editorial Eye*, March 1999. Alexandria, VA: EEI Press.

[2]Lindsell-Roberts, Sheryl. *Business Writing for Dummies.* New York: IDG Books Worldwide, 1999, p. 90.

[3]"Testing Your Documents." <www.plainlanguage.gov/howto/test.htm>

[4]Ibid.

[5]Kimble, Joseph. "Answering the Critics of Plain Language." *The Scribes Journal of Legal Writing* (1994-1995). <plainlanguage.gov/library/kimble.htm>

PART II

Types of Business Writing

CHAPTER 8

Emailing the Right Message

Email: Do the Old Rules Still Apply?

Mary wanted to request a five-day class in HTML (Hypertext Markup Language) for her administrative assistant, Anne. She decided to email the request to her boss, Chris. To organize her email, she wrote down all the reasons she could think of to support her request. She wanted to highlight Anne's accomplishments and show how the training would benefit both Anne and the division. Mary also knew that her boss would be concerned about a regional meeting for which Anne had a major planning responsibility. The meeting was coming up in January, and the HTML class was scheduled for early December. Mary wanted to alleviate any concerns that the class would interfere with Anne's responsibilities.

Some of the ideas she jotted down were:

- Anne needs the training to help with the agency's Web site.
- Regional meeting is in January, but planning is 80% complete.
- Can get temporary replacement for Anne.
- Anne has good attendance record.
- She does a lot in the office.
- She's taking on some of Tim's responsibilities for maintaining the Web site.
- HTML class is Dec. 5-9.
- Anne has handled travel details for participants competently in the past.
- Anne has organized a mailing list.

- She's been an administrative assistant here for five years.
- Evidence that Web site needs updating—it hasn't been touched in 3 months.
- December is typically a slack time in our office.

However, the ideas needed to be organized, with the main idea—the purpose for writing and her position—at the beginning. After much thought, Mary wrote the following email:

TO: Chris Thompson
FROM: Mary James
DATE: October 22, 2001
SUBJECT: Training Request for Anne Brown

I'm writing to request permission for Anne Brown to attend an HTML class December 5-9, 2001. She's asked for the training so that she can help update the Web site.

Need for Training
- Anne will be taking on some of Tim's responsibilities in maintaining our Web site.
- She cannot take on Tim's job until she learns HTML.
- The Web site has not been updated for 3 months.
- No one else in the office has the time to take on this job.

Anne's Record
As Anne's supervisor, I have noticed the following about her work:
- Her attendance record is excellent.
- She handles a variety of tasks, from writing reports and Web site copy to helping with the budget, with competence and careful attention to detail.
- She's been an administrative assistant here for five years and has requested training only once before.

The Annual Regional Meeting: No Problem

Anne is responsible for planning the annual regional meeting in January, but I do not believe that the HTML class will interfere with those responsibilities for the following reasons:

- She already has completed 80% of what needs to be done.
- She has organized a mailing list.
- She has the time to handle travel details both before and after the HTML class.
- December is a slack period in our department, and we can manage with a temporary replacement.

Thank you for your consideration of this. Please let me know if you have any questions.

An email message is a type of memorandum, but it has its own unique flavor. Memoranda formerly were handwritten on paper and distributed within an organization. While email is the preferred medium for intraorganizational correspondence, it also is used to communicate with customers, contractors, and others. An email message can range from an informal one-sentence request or statement to a multi-page, confidential analysis of critical policy issues.

When decisions, directives, orders, and other official news must reach many people at several levels within the organization, email provides an efficient vehicle. Even when a message must reach only one person or a small group, sending an email is often wise. An email is a reliable means of:

- Giving specific instructions

- Conveying detailed facts or figures

- Replying directly to another person's written or oral request

- Going on the record to establish that certain things have been said or done, or that certain views are held.

> Email overwhelms 60% of executives, managers, and other workplace professionals, according to a Pitney Bowes-funded workplace study.
>
> In an Ernst & Young poll, 36% of respondents reported using email more frequently than any other communication tool, including the telephone.[1]

Because email is easy and quick, it's a popular favorite in the workplace. However, many people think they do not need to use proper grammar or spelling in email messages. Electronic messages are still a form of communication that deserves careful thought, planning, and review.

In this chapter, we discuss how to organize and compose email. In Chapter 10, we discuss how to write informal reports, which sometimes are sent as email.

PLANNING EMAIL

Even when the email you wish to write is short and informal, you should resist the temptation to skip over the planning and outlining stage. As the previous case study shows, careful planning can turn jumbled thoughts into a well-written, organized message. When you need to send an important email:

1. Take the time to determine your purpose.

2. Assemble any helpful materials (earlier emails, other correspondence, policy statements, regulations, or other documents). Review them before you write.

3. Jot down key facts and note ideas that come to you.

4. Group the facts and ideas that belong together and establish a logical order of presentation.

ELEMENTS OF EMAIL

Emails usually include the following elements:

- *Heading.* The heading includes the following topics:
  - *To:*
  - *Copy:* (if copies are being distributed to other people)
  - *From:*
  - *Subject:*
  - *Sent* (date and time)
  - *Importance* (urgent, normal, etc.)

- *Body.*

The most important parts of the email are the *subject statement* and the *opening statement.*

Subject Statement

The subject statement is an opportunity to alert the reader immediately to the essence of the email. It should:

- Use only the words necessary to convey the subject clearly.

  "Subject: Results of Work Habits Survey"

- Use words that will get readers' attention.

  "Subject: Need for Immediate Decision on Flexitime Policy"

- Use names, titles, dates, and other details where helpful.

  "Subject: Transfer of James L. Jenkins from Planning and Scheduling to Research, Effective March 1, 20xx"

- Be broad enough to summarize what is covered but specific enough to highlight the main purpose.

  "Subject: Policy Order XX-XXX—Results of Our Analysis"

- Use language that readers will understand—technical terms or lay person's terms, as appropriate.

Opening Statement

The first paragraph of the email—preferably the first sentence—should tell why you are writing. State your position or convey the information. Don't make the reader dig to find out what the point is. And don't begin with filler phrases like "The purpose of this email is...." Get right to the point:

> "I recommend that we adopt the Type A Meetings Procedure described in Bill's March 29 letter."
>
> "We should expand this office to provide space for the seven new employees."
>
> "The new copy machine is inadequate for this office."
>
> "The director approved our proposal for revised accounting procedures."
>
> "Attached is the information you requested on the public's response to the updated form."

Well-written Email

- Saves time and avoid misunderstanding

- Contributes to the efficiency of the organization

- Enhances the reputation of the person who wrote it.

EMAIL ETIQUETTE (NETIQUETTE)

While many of the standard rules and niceties apply to emails, a few new ones have cropped up to meet the particular needs of this new type of communication.

Tone and Style

All the writing principles that apply to letters apply equally to email. Adapt your degree of formality to fit the expectations of the intended reader(s) and your purpose. In communicating an official policy, for example, you would want to be far more authoritative, impersonal, and serious than you would in addressing a request to a co-worker.

Use positive words whenever possible, and keep your messages courteous, direct, and brief. Unlike face-to-face communication, written messages cannot be modified by body language and tone of voice. Because of this, they are often misinterpreted. Also, be aware of the recipient's style and try to adapt your style accordingly. For example, if the recipient sends you a long, effusive email, you do not want to send back a curt, three-word reply.

On the other hand, *if you want the recipient of the email to take action, be sure to state what that action is and when you would like it to occur.* Use tact and consideration in framing the request, but be direct and specific about what you want or need.

The Right Recipients and the Right Timing

Communicating to the right person at the right time is just as important when sending an email as it is when sending a letter.

- Send your message to the right person. Make sure your email goes to the person responsible for the activity or function. Do not go over anyone's head. If you do not get results, you should tell the person that you plan to take the matter up with someone in higher authority.

- Send copies to the right people. Send copies of an email to anyone affected by the subject or interested in it. Also send copies to anyone mentioned in the email, and anyone in a direct line of authority between you and the addressee. Do not waste peoples' time by sending office-wide emails on topics that do not concern most employees.

- Avoid surprising your reader. Prepare your reader for surprising news, especially if it is negative. Call ahead to explain, "You'll be getting an email later today to explain why your budget was cut."

- Send important information to the important people first. Not everyone reads email when it first arrives. Consider sending critical information a day or so ahead to the key people or to those who would be embarrassed if they did not know about it before the others.

Other Guidelines

Other tips helpful in writing emails include:

- Avoid "screaming." Do not write your email using all capital letters, as this is the email equivalent of screaming.

- Don't designate a message urgent unless it *is* urgent. If something is urgent, consider phoning rather than risking that the recipient won't see it in time.

- Inform email recipients when your message does not require a reply. You can simply add "FYI—no reply needed" to these messages.

- Keep attachments to a minimum. The larger the attached document, the longer it takes to download and the more memory space it fills on the recipient's computer. Also, many people are wary of attachments because of the possibility of viruses. If you need to send an attachment, it's a good idea to alert the recipient ahead of time.

- Reduce the number of "Thanks!" replies. Such "content-free mail" is not necessary unless (1) the thank-you is really called for, or (2) you need to let the sender know you received the message.

- Know when not to write. Highly sensitive or very personal messages are often better communicated in person or "off the record." Do not send any message in the heat of anger, and avoid critical, gossipy, or sarcastic messages.

SECURITY AND PRIVACY ISSUES

Nothing is private. Even when messages are deleted, they can be accessed on the hard drive by software or online services. Before you click Send, think about the consequences of someone other than the intended recipient—like your boss—reading the message.

- Employers feel they have the right to know if you're using their email system for personal messages and they sometimes check email.

- The U.S. government often monitors its messages to protect against email that is being sent for illegal purposes.

TEST YOURSELF: STATING THE SUBJECT AND PURPOSE

Give each email a more informative subject statement. Then write a one-sentence or two-sentence opening that makes the purpose clear. Suggested answers can be found in the Appendix on page 315.

SUBJECT: Hiring

This email will forward to you a copy of a new directive spelling out in detail this company's equal employment opportunity policy. Also attached is a copy of the Equal Opportunity Employment Law. In brief, the directive makes clear that this company hires people solely on merit; no applicant will be turned down because of race, religion, or sex. As you know, equal opportunity employment has been an understood policy of this company for many years. We now make this policy official through the attached directive.

SUBJECT:

(Opening)

SUBJECT: Recent Staff Meeting

(This summary is based on my rough notes during our meeting on October 24. If I have left out something or haven't accurately reflected something we agreed on, please let me know right away.)

We discussed the issue of employee career development at length. We then agreed that we should take the steps that I have outlined below:

Our Training and Development Committee will study innovative methods of promoting employee career development.

John will review our present employee career development activities.

We will hold a follow-up meeting on November 9 to review the findings of these efforts.

SUBJECT:

(Opening)

TEST YOURSELF: WRITING A SHORT EMAIL

Your division chief likes to be kept informed in writing of critical events and what you're doing about them. He likes to-the-point emails that he can follow up on later by phone. You are an enforcement officer for a government agency, and you've been planning to send four of your staff to inspect conditions at the Cotton Comfortwear Mill. The inspection is authorized and required by Code Sections XXXXX through XXXXX. The inspection will last three days: August 4, 5, and 6. It was scheduled, and Cotton Comfortwear was informed, more than three months ago.

This morning, you have learned that the mill operators have filed papers in court to keep you off their property. They have also directed some rather offensive, although not threatening, remarks to you by telephone over the past few weeks. You have told your inspection team to "stay the hell out of" the plant until you get further instructions from your division chief and the legal branch.

Write the subject statement and the body of a brief email to the division chief.

SUBJECT:

A suggested version can be found in the Appendix on page 316.

Despite its ease of use, electronic mail requires careful thought, planning, and review. Email is an efficient method for communicating with many people in several levels of an organization. It also is often the medium of choice for communicating with only one person or a small group, as well as with customers, contractors, and others. An email message can range from an informal one-sentence request or statement to a multi-page, confidential analysis of critical policy issues.

The most important parts of an email message are the subject line and the opening statement. The subject statement should alert the reader immediately to the essence of the email. It should be broad enough to summarize what is covered but specific enough to highlight the main purpose. The opening statement presents the purpose of the email, its importance to the reader, and the writer's position. Conclusions and recommendations should follow the opening statement.

Email etiquette is important to follow. Adapt your tone and style to the purpose of the email. If you want the reader to take action, make sure you state what that action is and when it should be completed. By respecting the rights and the schedules of others, you can send emails when necessary to the right people and avoid sending unnecessary mail.

Before sending an email message, think about the consequences of someone else reading it. Employers, including the U.S. government, often monitor employee messages.

---

[1]Abernathy, Donna. "You've Got Email." *Training and Development.* April 1999, p. 18.

CHAPTER 9

Writing Winning Letters

When Tact Is Required

Jane was in a dilemma. She needed to write a letter thanking the man who spoke at the monthly meeting. Unfortunately, he was a flop. His talk was poorly organized, he had technical problems with his slide show, and he bored his listeners.

"What can I do?" she asked Lee.

"You need to acknowledge the effort and thank him tactfully without exaggerating his talents," said Lee.

Jane worked for a while then showed Lee the results.

Dear Robert,

We want to thank you for the considerable time and expertise that went into your special presentation at our monthly meeting. It was greatly appreciated.

We can't hear your message about government ethics too often, and you gave our people much to think about. Your energy in the face of technical problems was admirable, especially in the difficult after-lunch time slot.

Please accept our gratitude for your hard work and dedication. Thank you again, very much.

Best Regards,
Jane Doe

"That's just right for a one-time effort that went wrong," said Lee. "If you plan to have Robert speak again, I would follow this letter with some face-to-face advice on how to improve performance."[1]

Every good letter you write will help your organization build good relations with the public and with other organizations. Thank-you letters, for example, are good etiquette and should be sent to anyone who does something for you, even if they are paid. In other cases, a letter is often the first contact—and may be the only contact—a person has with your organization.

Melodee Mercer, a Veterans Benefits Administration (VBA) administrator who helped the agency shift to "reader-focused writing," says writing shapes the public's perception of the government, good or bad. "People have often thought of government employees as robots. You get what you give," Mercer says. "If you write like a robot, people will think of you as a robot."

VBA staff have found that improving correspondence allows the agency to serve veterans more efficiently. As VBA employees have changed the way they communicate, veterans are writing fewer complaint letters and many more thank-you letters. This chapter contains several examples that show how VBA letters now focus on the reader. In this chapter, we show how to write a clear, well-organized, and persuasive letter.

THE IMPORTANCE OF ORGANIZATION

Good organization saves time—for *you* and *your reader*.

You can write the letter right the first time. You won't have to spend time crossing out repetitions or unnecessary remarks, or inserting a key idea you left out the first time.

Your reader will get the message at first reading, rather than backtracking to trace the thread of meaning through a maze of thought.

Most readers:

- Are constantly interrupted by meetings, phone calls, lunch, or even business trips as they attempt to read your document

- Want you to get to the point quickly

- Will ask themselves:

  —Why should I read this?

  —What's this about? What's the point of it?

  —What's in this for me?

  —What am I being asked to do?

BASIC STEPS IN WRITING BUSINESS LETTERS

Following a few basic rules will help you in writing business letters:

Rule 1. *Determine your purpose.* Are you writing to inform or to persuade? Plan before you write.

Rule 2. *Identify your audience.* Think about the role, attitude, and background information the reader has.

Rule 3. *Know your subject.* Review correspondence and other information and talk to anyone who can provide additional information.

Rule 4. *Put the message in sequence.* Present your ideas in a logical order. Organize your letter according to your purpose.

Rule 5. *Immediately identify the subject and give your position.* Explain why you are writing in the first paragraph—or in the first sentence, if you can. Let your readers know why they should read the letter and what your position is.

Rule 6. *Create a paragraph for each step in the process.* Keep paragraphs short. Use headings and subparagraphs to make the structure clear.

Rule 7. *Include only what your reader must know to understand, agree, or act.* Use enough detail to make things clear, but not so much that the reader loses the big picture.

Rule 8. *End by pointing the way ahead.* Tell the reader what is to happen next.

HOW TO BEGIN THE LETTER

Get right to the point! Many business writers ignore this principle. Some mumble for a while before they get to the main idea:

> "The object of this letter is to ask your cooperation regarding one of your former employees who has now applied for employment with this agency. We would much appreciate it if...."

Others start off with a meaningless acknowledgment:

> "We have received the form you sent us by return mail earlier this month."

Instead, tell the reader immediately why you are writing:

> "This letter is to inform you that Section 6 of the St. George's Hundred Project has not been accepted by the James City Service Authority for the following reasons:"

"The Master Plan for St. Thomas' Hundred Project was approved by the Planning Commission on February 5, 2000."

Give a Point of Reference

If you are answering a message from your reader, it is a good idea to give the reader a point of reference. But don't bore the reader with irrelevant detail. Instead, use a brief reference line:

"Re: Your letter of April 30, 20xx"

"Re: Application Form XXX-XX-XX"

Or, refer to the topic of the reader's previous message in the first sentence of your letter.

"I am pleased to inform you that your June 15, 20xx, application has been approved by our evaluation branch."

An Exception: Say No Slowly

There is one exception to the principle of stating your purpose in the first paragraph. When your message is likely to be distasteful or disappointing to the reader (that is, when you have to say no), you may want to let the facts speak first, and then state the purpose. In other words, you may want to put the bad news at or near the end of the message. In this way, you prepare the reader for the worst—or present your evidence first to help prevent any further argument.

The following is a sample of a "no" letter:

Thank you for your adoption application.

The number of infants available for adoption has greatly decreased in the past few years. As a result, all state-operated adoption agencies continue to receive requests from many more families than they have babies to place. The need for homes for older, handicapped, and minority children has increased, and agencies are primarily seeking adoptive families for these special-need groups. At the present time, we have many applications from families interested only in infants. We are therefore not accepting additional families for consideration because we cannot be confident about placing an infant in the home within a reasonable period of time. The district office will keep your inquiry on file and will consider you along with other families when it is able to accept more families for study.

While I am sorry to disappoint you, I hope this information will be helpful in understanding the current adoption situation.[2]

HOW TO ORGANIZE THE BODY OF THE LETTER

In the body of your letter, you give information to support the position you stated in the first paragraph. For example, if you are trying to convince upper management to adopt a revised flexitime policy (a letter of persuasion), you would give your reasons and the data that support your reasons in the body of your letter.

The Inverted Pyramid

Chapter 2 suggested some methods for organizing documents. The method of organization you choose will depend upon the type of information you are presenting. However, for most letters, the inverted pyramid is an ideal structure. In this structure, the most important idea goes first (the broad top of the inverted pyramid), the second most important idea next, and so on.

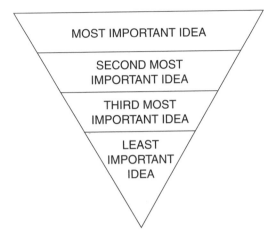

The inverted pyramid structure is the model for news writing. Journalism students learn early on that it is best to organize newspaper articles with the most important information first. There are two reasons for this: newspaper readers and newspaper editors.

Newspaper readers often do not read more than the headline and the first few paragraphs. Putting the "who, what, where, when, why, and how" up front gives the busy reader the basic information he or she wants and allows the reader to decide whether to read further for more details.

Newspaper editors, knowing that readers don't read every word and that information should be arranged in an inverted pyramid, often cut articles from the bottom up to fit the available space.

When You Are Writing to More Than One Audience

You may be talking to exporters and importers, coal miners and surface owners, or airlines and passengers. Break your letter down into essential elements and determine which elements apply to each part of your audience. Then group the elements according to who is affected. You might create a table for this purpose to help the reader find pertinent information.

The *Plain Language Action Network* gives an example of how to address more than one audience:

(a) When you apply for a grant, you must send us:

  (1) A description of your experience in the area covered by the grant; and

  (2) Copies of any material that you have published relevant to the area of the grant.

(b) Your financial office must send us:

  (1) The name and address of the chief financial officer;

  (2) A description of the in-kind match you will provide;

  (3) Your approved overhead rate; and

  (4) A proposed budget.

HOW TO END THE LETTER

The ending of your letter answers the question, "What next?" You tell what you want your readers to do, what you plan to do, or you just end with a thank you, apology, etc.

What Readers Should Do

Tell your readers what you want them to do.

> "If I can be of further help, please let me know by (calling or writing). . . ."

> "Please call me collect to tell me your decision."

What You Intend to Do

Or tell them what you plan to do:

"I'll be getting in touch with you next week."

"If you approve this plan, I will call and get bids from the three companies next week."

Or Just End

Occasionally, you might just say:

"Thank you for bringing this matter to our attention."

"Thank you."

"We regret any inconvenience that we might have caused you."

Never present new ideas or raise new issues in ending a letter. If you hint about topics that you haven't discussed, you will only bewilder and frustrate your reader.

WRITING LETTERS FOR SPECIFIC PURPOSES

Most often, you will be writing letters for a particular reason.

Letters of Persuasion

On occasion, you may need to write a letter asking the recipient(s) to do something—recycle motor oil, use child safety seats, or send in a form, for example. When you need to write a letter of persuasion, it's a good idea to follow the model used for sales letters:

- *Open* with a device to get the reader's attention:

  —involve the reader in some way

  —offer a benefit

  —make a startling statement or present a surprising statistic

  —ask a rhetorical question.

- Use the *body* of the letter to:

  —show how the proposal will benefit the reader

  —explain exactly what you have in mind

  —emphasize the main features of the proposal.

- Near the *end* of the letter:

  —ask the reader for a specific action

  —remind the reader of the benefit

  —create a sense of urgency.

- Make your writing positive and energetic *throughout.*

Later we discuss how to compose a budget justification statement, which is similar to a letter of persuasion.

"IRAC" (Issue, Rule, Application, Conclusion) System of Legal Writing

Regardless of whether you must write legal letters, it is useful to know how to use the IRAC system of writing. This technique is used whenever you need to apply a rule or regulation to a specific situation.

This following example shows how to use the IRAC system.

Issue   Did Sam Ware violate agency ethics regulations when he accepted free tuition to a professional conference on the latest trends in government procurement?

Rule   Ethics Rule 2.1 prohibits acceptance of any gratuity by a government employee from an organization seeking to do business with the government.

Application Sam Ware's action involved acceptance of a gratuity. The course tuition had a dollar value of $325 and the conference sponsor was an organization seeking to do business with his agency.

Conclusion   Sam Ware violated ethics regulations and is therefore subject to discipline.[3]

Letters of Recommendation

Nearly everyone is asked to write a letter of recommendation at one time or another. The following are some guidelines:

1. Review a copy of the applicant's personal statement or application essays so that your letter of recommendation can dovetail with—not conflict with or duplicate—the rest of the application.

2. Ask the applicant to supply you with additional information such as a resume.

3. Describe your qualifications for comparing the applicant to other applicants:

"I have personally supervised 10 interns every summer for the last 5 years in addition to working with more than 200 college graduates in my capacity as training officer for the Recreation Department."

4. Discuss how well you know the applicant:

"Mr. Jones reported to me directly for two years prior to his well-deserved promotion to the position of Manager in the Travel Office."

5. Choose two or three qualities that you observed in the applicant.

"Ms. Tyler has made an outstanding contribution to the field of medicine and has a rare blend of good communication skills and analytical abilities."

6. In discussing these qualities, support your statements with specific instances in which the person demonstrated those attributes. Be as concrete and detailed as possible.

"Because of Derek's writing skills, I did not hesitate to ask him to write a report that was used by our office as the basis of a major policy statement. Congressmember Jones eventually used that statement, based on Derek's sophisticated 20-page analysis of Middle East politics, in lobbying for increased funding."

7. Try to quantify the person's strengths or compare him or her to other employees that you have observed:

"She has the best analytical skills of any person her age that I have ever supervised."

8. Discuss the applicant's potential in his or her chosen field.

"I enthusiastically recommend Mr. Johnson to your business school. This well-rounded employee will be a fine business-person."[4]

Letters Accompanying Reports

When you have a report attached, you write a brief letter letting the reader know what the report is about. The following is an example:

Dear Federal employee,

During this past fiscal year, OPM reached out to the human resources community to assess how well we are meeting the needs of our customers. We developed two customer satisfaction surveys: one for human resources directors and one for human resources specialists. We received responses from 43 HR directors and 1,340 HR specialists in the field and headquarters.

Each survey primarily asked our customers to rate OPM's policy leadership; our efforts to involve agencies in policy development; how well OPM provides technical assistance; and how effectively we are sharing technical information. On the next two pages you will find some of the key findings from the survey data which reflect evaluations of all of OPM's program areas. While we are pleased that many of the responses indicated high levels of satisfaction, there are areas where we need improvement. This is the first time that OPM has received a comprehensive "report card" from our customers and we are excited at the prospect of working with the human resources community to make our service even better.

Janice Lachance
Director
Office of Personnel Management

FORMATTING YOUR LETTERS TO INCREASE EFFECTIVENESS

Many techniques can be used to format your letters in a way that gets your message across most effectively.

Using Indented Lists

Listing your points either through enumeration or bulleting can make a series of items clearer and more convincing. However, the items in a list should be related to one another in a clear way and should be well organized. The following are guidelines for lists:

1. *Lists must contain items of the same classification.* To create an effective list, you must sort your information into appropriate categories. You should not mix causes and effects, for example.

2. *Lists must have parallel construction.* Lists must have the same grammatical construction and begin with the same part of speech. For example, if the first point in the list is a complete sentence, every other point in the list must be a complete sentence. If the first point begins with an infinitive (such as "to begin"), every other point in the list must begin with an infinitive.

Using Headings

Headings are subjects or titles for sections of your document. They are signposts that help your reader follow what you are saying.

What Headings Do

Headings should do more than simply indicate the part of the document in which the readers have found themselves, e.g., "Introduction," "Chapter 1." Headings should also summarize the main points of those sections, much like a newspaper headline, e.g., "Introduction: Average Credit Card Debt at Record High as Savings Rates Fall."

Like your paragraphs, your headings will notify readers when you move from one topic to another.

Headings also break up what can be the unremitting grayness of the text. Make sure that you include a heading or subheading every few pages. Spence recommends that you use two headings per single-spaced page to break the text of documents that are more than one page.[5]

The following are some tips for writing headings:

1. *Brainstorm* for words, phrases, or questions that best pinpoint your topic. Don't hesitate to rewrite your headings a few times. It's worth the effort. To compose an effective heading, ask yourself, "What am I going to say in this section?"

2. *Make headings specific and accurate.* Try to give more information, rather than less. Readers should be able to get the gist of a document and see your logic at a glance by reading the headings in the table of contents.

3. *Use an action verb* whenever you can. "Hire a Staff Accountant" is better than "Staff Accountant."

4. Be sure to *use the active voice.* Use "Recommendations Improve Employee Training" rather than "Employee Training Improved by Recommendations."

5. *Be sure they flow* in a logical sequence and that they cover all of your main points.

6. Like items in a list, *headings should be parallel.* For example, all of the following headings begin with an *–ing* verb:

— Opening a Document File

— Creating a Data Base

— Revising Data Base Entries

— Exporting Files to Other Programs

— Consulting the System Dictionary

— Checking for Errors and Inconsistencies

Make the Headings Long Enough to be Descriptive

Instead of:	Write:
Overview	How Staff Attorneys Can Benefit From Using the LAWNET Data Base
Accounting Report	2000 Versus 1999 Annual Revenues
Business Plan	A Proposed Schedule for Opening Three New Branch Offices

---

How Headings Can Help

Headings can help make a letter clearer, especially if the letter is long and/or complex. The following are two versions of the same letter, the first *without* headers and the second *with* headers.[6]

Letter Written in Traditional Format

VETERANS BENEFITS ADMINISTRATION

Change in Enrollment Status

Addressee:

Street:

City:

State/zip:

Dear addressee:

This letter regards the change in your enrollment status during the term that began September 1, 1996. If the change was due to unavoidable events beyond your control, please notify us as soon as possible. Otherwise, you may be held responsible for an overpayment, or an additional overpayment of benefits.

When giving the reasons for your enrollment change, be as specific as possible. Explain what interfered with your enrollment, give important dates (such as the beginning and ending dates of an illness), and state how your enrollment was affected. In most cases, we will be able to accept your reason only if you submit supporting evidence (such as a doctor's certification to verify an illness, a statement from your employer to confirm a required change in work schedule, etc.).

If you show sufficient grounds for making this enrollment change, any necessary reduction or termination of your award will be effective no earlier than the date your enrollment status actually changed. If your evidence does not establish the change was caused by unanticipated circumstances beyond your control, or if you do not respond within 30 days, your award must be reduced to the rate of $0 effective the first day of the term in which the change took place.

You withdrew from one or more courses on November 5, 1996. Currently, your award has been reduced effective December 1, 1996. You will receive a computer-generated letter with more details, including the amount of overpayment, if any. If you do not provide acceptable reasons for this course change, your check due on or about January 1 may be reduced or not issued at all due to an additional overpayment.

You will be notified when the decision is made on your case.

Letter with Headings

VETERANS BENEFITS ADMINISTRATION

Change in Enrollment Status

addressee

street

city

state/zip

Dear addressee:

This letter is about the change in your enrollment during the period that began on September 1, 1996. Because of this change, we may have paid you more than you were due.

What Our Records Show

You reduced your credit hours from 12 hours to 6 hours on November 5, 1996.

What We Did

We reduced your payments on December 1, 1996 to $202.00 per month. You will receive another letter about this change. The letter will show if you have a debt.

What We Need

Please send us a statement explaining why you reduced the number of your credit hours. In most cases, we require evidence to support your statement. If you do not have supporting evidence, please tell us why. (See the enclosure Changes in Your Enrollment.)

When We Need It

Send us your statement with any supporting evidence within 30 days.

What We Will Do

If we accept your statement, we will not reduce your payments from the beginning date of the term. If a debt has already been created, it must be repaid, but the debt will not be increased.

If we do not accept your statement with supporting evidence, we will reduce your payments on September 1, 1996, the beginning date of the term. This will create a debt that you must repay.

If you do not respond within 30 days, we will reduce your payments on September 1, 1996, the beginning date of the term. This will create a debt that you must repay. Although we will take this action, we will consider information received from you within one year from the date of this letter. (We may extend this time limit if you show a good reason why you could not meet it.)

Your Rights

You have basic rights that are available to you before we make a final decision on your claim. (See the enclosure Basic Rights.)

Sincerely,

Enclosures:

VA Form 21-4138

Changes in Your Enrollment

Basic Rights

If You Need Help

TEST YOURSELF: WRITING A LETTER USING HEADINGS

Rewrite the following letter using headings:[7]

VETERANS BENEFITS ADMINISTRATION

Pension Medical Evidence

Addressee:

Street:

City:

State/zip:

Dear addressee:

Please furnish medical evidence in support of your pension claim. The best evidence to submit would be a report of a recent examination by your personal physician, or a report from a hospital or clinic that has treated you recently. The report should include complete findings and diagnoses of the condition that renders you permanently and totally disabled. It is not necessary for you to receive an examination at this time. We only need a report from a doctor, hospital, or clinic that has treated you recently.

This evidence should be submitted as soon as possible, preferably within 60 days. If we do not receive this information within 60 days from the date of this letter, your claim will be denied. Evidence must be received in the Department of Veterans Affairs within one year from the date of this letter; otherwise, benefits, if entitlement is established, may not be paid prior to the date of its receipt.

SHOW VETERAN'S FULL NAME AND VA FILE NUMBER ON ALL EVIDENCE SUBMITTED.

Privacy Act Information: The information requested by this letter is authorized by existing law (38 U.S.C. 210 (c) (1)) and is considered necessary and relevant to determine entitlement to maximum benefits applied for under the law. The information submitted may be disclosed outside the Department of Veterans Affairs only as permitted by law.

Sincerely,

Suggested revised letter can be found in the Appendix, page 317.

Using a Question-and-Answer Format

The reader comes to your letter with questions that he or she needs answered. It's much more efficient to anticipate the reader's questions and pose them as he or she would. By doing this, you make it easier for the reader to find information.

Since the question-and-answer format assumes that the reader is the one asking the questions, use "I" in questions to refer to the reader. In responses, your organization (represented by "we") addresses the reader.

The following table shows an older version of a regulation with short headings that did not help the reader with specific information. On the right are the rewritten headings, formatted to fit the reader's needs.

Sample Question-and-Answer Format

Special Grants for Economic Development and Core Management Grants to Small Tribes	*Economic Development and Core Management Grants to Small Tribes*
§ 254.11 Indian Rights	§ 254.11 How do the procedures in this part affect Indian rights?
§ 254.12 Applications	§ 254.12 How do I apply for a grant under this part?
§254.13 Multi-tribal Grants	§ 254.13 When must I submit my application?
§254.14 Administrative Requirements	§ 254.14 Can a multi-tribal organization submit a single grant request?
§254.15 Appeals	§ 254.15 What special information is required for an application by a multi-tribal organization?

Using "If-Then" Tables

If material is particularly complex and many conditional situations are involved, put an if-then table in your letter. Tables help your reader see relationships in a way that dense text never can. No one would dispute that the rewritten regulation below is far clearer than the dense text it replaces.

Before

§ 163.25 Forest management deductions.

(a) Pursuant to the provisions of 25 USC 413 and 25 USC 3105, a forest management deduction shall be withheld from the gross proceeds of sales of Indian forest land as described in this section.

(b) Gross proceeds shall mean the value in money or money's worth of consideration furnished by the purchaser of forest products purchased under a contract, permit, or other document for the sale of forest products.

(c) Forest management deductions shall not be withheld where the total consideration furnished under a document for the sale of forest products is less than $5,001.

(d) Except as provided in § 163.25 (e) of this part, the amount of the forest deduction shall not exceed the lesser amount of ten percent (10%) of the gross proceeds or, the actual percentage in effect on November 28, 1990.

(e) The Secretary may increase the forest management deduction percentage for Indian forest land upon receipt of a written request from a tribe supported by a written resolution executed by the authorized tribal representatives. At the request of the authorized tribal representatives and at the discretion of the Secretary the forest management deduction percentage may be decreased to not less than one percent (1%) or the requirement for collection may be waived.[1]

After

§ 163.25 What forest management deductions will BIA withhold?

We will withhold a forest management deduction if the contract for the sale of forest products has a value of over $5,000. The deduction will be a percentage of the gross proceeds (i.e., the price we get from the buyer). We will determine the amount of the deduction in accordance with the following table.

If . . .	Then the percentage of the deduction is . . .
a tribe requests an increase in the deduction through a tribal resolution and written request to us	the percentage requested by the tribe.
an authorized tribal representative requests and we approve a decrease in the deduction	the percentage requested, with a 1% minimum.
an authorized tribal representative requests and we approve a waiver of the deduction	waived.
none of the above conditions apply	the percentage in effect on November 28, 1990, or 10 percent, whichever is less.

TEST YOURSELF: CREATING AN IF-THEN TABLE

Create an if-then table using the information below:

§ 163.17 Deposit with bid.

(a) A deposit shall be made with each proposal for the purchase of Indian forest products. Such deposits shall be at least:

(1) Ten (10) percent if the appraised stumpage value is less than $100,000 and in any event not less than $1,000 or full value whichever is less;

(2) Five (5) percent if the appraised stumpage value is $100,000 to $250,000 but in any event not less than $10,000; and

(b) Three (3) percent if the appraised stumpage value exceeds $250,000 but in any event not less than $12,500.

A suggested answer can be found in the Appendix, page 318.

Well-written letters are a reflection on both you and your organization. Letters should be clearly organized and directed to the specific audience(s) to which they are addressed. Give the main point of the letter first, unless you are conveying bad news.

Use headings to share your structure with the reader and serve as signposts. Use specific, accurate headings with active verbs. Make sure the headings are parallel and that they flow logically.

Using a question-and-answer format in your letter helps the reader find the information needed. Likewise, if-then tables guide a reader through a document, especially a complex one with many conditional situations.

---

[1]Adapted from Basye, Anne. *Business Letters Ready to Go!* Lincolnwood, IL: NTC Business Books, 1998, p. 110. Used with permission.

[2]Paxson, William C. *The Business Writing Handbook.* New York, Bantam Books, 1981.

[3]Rider, Donald G. *Effective Writing for Feds,* Huntsville, AL: FPMI Communications, 1992.

[4]www.accepted.com/mba/letter_rec.htm. Copyright © Accepted. com™ 1996-2000. Used with permission.

[5]Spence, Padraic. *Business Writing:The Good, the Bad, and the Ugly.* Stockbridge, MA: The Water Street Press, 1996. P. 112.

[6]Adapted from *Writing User-Friendly Documents.* <www.plain language.gov>

[7]This is an actual "before" letter taken from *Writing User-Friendly Documents.* <www.plainlanguage.gov.> The answer is the "after" version.

CHAPTER 10

Creating Rousing Reports

Conveying Information Professionally

Jane and Tom had a chance to talk during lunch. The conversation led to their writing projects.

"What advice can you give me about writing reports?" asked Tom. "I have a report to write on last month's site visits."

"Well, remember, although reports are not as conversational as letters," Jane said, "you want your report to convey a friendly, but professional tone.

"Also, reports need to be definite and specific. Don't qualify your statements with phrases like 'I think maybe' or 'in most cases' unless you feel you have to. And whenever you can, back up your statements with evidence or examples. For example, here's a paragraph from a report I just received from our Research Office:

> We have concluded that the monthly visit approach works best. In the four months since we have been using it, we have been able to obtain twice as much useful information in less than half the time. While we used to spend an average of 24 hours a month, we now spend 10 or 11. The information we obtain is more useful because...—you get the gist."

"I see what you mean," said Tom. "That's very clear and precise. Thanks so much."

A report is an impartial, objective, planned presentation of facts. It should be logical, accurate, reliable, and easy to read.

Every year hundreds of thousands of government employees get involved in at least some phase of the study/report process. Some volunteer; others are summoned to the task. A number of tasks in government require reports. These include:

- Preparation of legislation

- Development of policies and procedures

- Staffing

- Program analysis

- Employee evaluation

- Job description

- Budget preparation

- Office design

- Workflow analysis

- Office organization

- Strategic planning

- Annual planning

- Public relations.

In this chapter, we discuss the formats for a number of different kinds of reports:

- Research reports

- Feasibility reports

- Progress reports

- Laboratory reports

- Test reports

- Trip reports

- Trouble reports

- Proposals

- Minutes of meetings.

These reports can be *informal* or *formal*, depending on their length and complexity.

BASIC PARTS OF AN INFORMAL OR BRIEF REPORT

An informal report might be communicated in the form of an email or a written memorandum. The elements of a good report fall into three categories:

- Opening (introduction)

- Unfolding (body)

- Closing (conclusion).

Tips for Opening

The opening statement, or introduction, should set the stage for what will follow. It should let the reader know what to expect and make the reader want to read on.

Three basic approaches to writing openings are to:

- Tell the reader what topics you will be discussing in the report and their significance to the reader (big picture)

- Let the reader know what you think about, or how you will approach, the topics you will be discussing (position statement)

- State conclusions and recommendations that you will then explain and discuss in the rest of the report.

You may also use a combination of these approaches. In any case, the opening should be no longer and no more complicated than necessary. And it should be written with your reader's needs and interests in mind.

Tips for Unfolding

The main purpose of the unfolding, or body, of the report is to describe or analyze. Here is where you present your data and background information.

- In *describing*, you attempt to tell a story. Examples are:

    —relating what has happened over the past month

    —detailing what you have observed about a particular problem situation

    —spelling out the steps involved in performing a task.

- In *analyzing*, you look more closely and make some sense of things. For example:

    —spelling out trends that you have noticed over the past month

—providing an explanation of why the problem situation has developed

—explaining why particular steps are taken in getting a job done.

Whether you use the description approach or the analysis approach, you should decide on a logical way to organize the report. Some common ways of organizing (discussed in Chapter 2) include:

- Inverted pyramid

- Order of familiarity

- Order of location (spatial or geographic order)

- Alphabetical order

- Chronological order

- Category order

- Inductive order

- List

- Order for comparison

- Deductive order

- Statement of reasons method

- Comparative advantages method

- Problem-solution method

- Most acceptable to least acceptable

- Comparison/contrast.

Tips for Closing

The closing of a report is crucial. Here is where you convey the thoughts and impressions you want to leave with your reader.

Three basic approaches are to:

- Give the reader a concise, "in a nutshell" summary of what you have said

- Make final recommendations

- Spell out actions you plan to take.

Again, you can use a combination of these approaches.

Like the opening, the closing should be to the point. Say what you have to say firmly and briefly. Also like the opening, the closing should be aimed directly at your reader. Ask yourself: What wrap-up would be most helpful, most understandable, and most convincing to my reader?

FORMAL REPORTS

Formal reports are generally lengthier than informal reports. They often are comprehensive accounts of major technical projects such as:

- Reports on new developments in a field

- Recommendations on whether to launch a new product or service

- Accounts of activities within the organization.

The length and complexity of the report depend upon the length and complexity of the project. Elements of formal reports include:

- Title page

- Any letters relevant to the report

- Executive summary (sometimes called abstract)

- Table of contents

- List of figures (if appropriate)

- List of tables

- List of abbreviations and symbols

- Acknowledgments, preface, or foreword

- Purpose of report—subject, scope, plan

- Background

- Policy statement

- Introduction

- Analysis and supporting data

- Conclusions

- Recommendations

- Final summary

- Glossary

- Appendices

- References

- Index.

Title Page

The title page should include:

- A title indicating the topic and the objective of the report (avoid using unfamiliar acronyms, and the self-evident phrase, "Report on ...")

- The writer's name

- The writer's organization

- The person or organization receiving the report

- The date.

Executive Summary

It is essential that any report of three pages or more contain a short, informative overview. The executive summary, sometimes called a "management overview," "preliminary summary," or "abstract," is perhaps *the* most important element of the report, because it may be the only part that is actually read. It states:

- The project's background

- The purpose and nature of the report

- The procedure for the study

- Budgetary implications

- Major findings and conclusions

- Recommendations.

The key to a successful summary is keeping it short (200 to 250 words or less) and informative. The executive summary is important for several reasons:

- Busy managers can—and often do—read the summary and skim the rest of the report. It is aimed at managers and others who do not have the technical background or the time to read the entire report.

- The executive summary may be the basis for acceptance or rejection of a report for publication or presentation.

- Executive summaries are the basis of computerized searches.

Executive summaries sometimes are placed immediately after the table of contents.

The following is an example of an executive summary.[1]

Sample Executive Summary

The City of Winslow hired McDuff, Inc., to perform a study of Wildwood Creek. The section of the creek that was studied is a one-mile-long area in Burns Nature Park, from Newell College to U.S. Highway 42. The study lasted seven months.

McDuff completed 13 tests on four different test dates. Wildwood scored fairly well on many of the tests, but there were some problem areas. For example, high levels of phosphates were uncovered in the water. The phosphates were derived either from fertilizer or from animal and plant matter and waste. Also uncovered were small amounts of undesirable water organisms that are tolerant to pollutants and can survive in harsh environments.

McDuff recommends that (1) the tests done in this study be conducted two more times, through spring 2002, (2) other environmental tests be conducted, as listed in the conclusions and recommendations section, and (3) a voluntary cleanup of the creek be scheduled. With these steps, we can better analyze the environmental integrity of Wildwood Creek.

Table of Contents

A well-organized, detailed table of contents makes it easy for the reader to identify all the elements in a document. Your table of contents should be a reliable road map that readers can follow to get through a process painlessly.

The table of contents below is organized in a logical sequence for a discretionary grant program. The organization follows the order in which events occur and the order in which the public might ask questions about the program.[2]

Sample Table of Contents

Part 791: Javits Gifted and Talented Students
Subpart A: How the Grant Program Works

Sec.

791.1   What is the Javits Gifted and Talented Students Education Program?

791.2   Am I eligible for a Javits Grant?

791.3   What activities are appropriate for Javits Grant funding?

791.4   What funding priorities may the Secretary establish?

791.5   What other regulations apply to the Javits Grant?

791.6   What definitions apply to the Javits Grant?

Subpart B: How to Apply for an Award

791.10   Where can I write to obtain a Javits Grant application?

791.11   What materials do I need to submit to be considered for a Javits Grant?

791.12   Where do I send my application?

791.13   When is my application due?

Subpart C: How the Secretary Makes an Award

791.20   How will the Secretary evaluate my application for a Javits Grant?

791.21   What selection criteria does the Secretary use to award Javits Grants?

791.22   Does the Secretary consider additional factors?

Subpart D: Grantees' Rights and Responsibilities

791.30   Under what conditions may I use my Javits Grant award?

791.31   What are my responsibilities for serving students and teachers in private schools?

The table of contents should:

- Indicate the headings in the report, with their page numbers

- Include all items in the report except itself and the title page.

List of Figures

Some writing experts recommend including a list of figures in reports with more than five illustrations (drawings, photographs, maps, charts, and graphs). The list of figures serves as a separate table of contents for these illustrations, which are numbered consecutively with Arabic numbers.

List of Tables

Some experts also recommend that a report with more than five tables contain a list of tables. This list serves as a separate table of contents for tables, which are numbered consecutively with Arabic numbers.

List of Abbreviations and Symbols

This list is useful if a report contains many abbreviations and symbols that may confuse the reader. List each symbol and each abbreviation in alphabetical order and tell what it stands for.

Body

The body is the complete account of the topic. It should cover the technical details and managerial implications.

Technical documents often rely on three elements of form within the body:

- Definitions

- Descriptions

- Instructions.

Analysis and Supporting Data

In this section of the report, you analyze your findings and present information that supports your position. To persuade your readers, you must present concrete evidence to back up your position. Follow these guidelines:

- Introduce only enough data to prove each issue. Do not overwhelm your readers.

- To be authoritative, be as concrete and specific as possible. Use numbers and percentages instead of such abstract phrases as "significant increase" or "substantial gain."

- Provide quotes or opinions from respected sources.

- Present tables and graphs.[3]

Conclusions

These are the deductions you draw from the data, your results. Your conclusions must prove your position by summarizing the implications of the data:

- Does the analysis show that my conclusions are correct?

- Are there factors that could affect the validity of my conclusions?

Recommendations

Finally, you tell readers what they are expected to do to put your position into effect and what you, the writer, will do to further your position.

Ask yourself:

- Will my recommendations improve the current situation?

- Do the advantages of my recommendations outweigh the disadvantages?

- Are there reasonable alternatives to my recommendation(s), and should I present them?

References

Any materials referred to or quoted from should be listed in a references section. References may take the form of:

- Footnotes (listed at the bottom of the page on which the reference appears)

- Endnotes (listed in a separate block section at the end of the chapter, section, or report).

In general, longer reports should have reference sections at the end of each section of the report.

Bibliography

The bibliography is a separate listing of all source materials used in researching the report but not cited in the text itself.

Appendices

Appendices contain information that supports or clarifies the report, but that is too detailed or voluminous to appear in the text without impeding the flow of ideas. This information might take the form of:

- Questionnaires used in the study

- Interviews used in the study

- Tabular results of the questionnaires and interviews

- Other data, presented in charts, graphs, and tables

- Correspondence.

Appendices are especially useful when your report is going to a diverse audience, some of whom may not want or need to read the information in the appendix. Generally, each type of material should have its own appendix. Appendices are usually labeled "Appendix A," "Appendix B," and so on.

Glossary

The glossary is an alphabetical listing of technical terms and their definitions, written in dictionary style. The terms selected will depend on the intended readers' background.

Index

The index is an alphabetical, cross-referenced list of all topics and subjects of importance in the report.

FORMATS FOR WORKPLACE REPORTS

The following are explanations of how to organize the more common types of business report. Following a set format for a business report can help the reader identify your purpose early on and pay attention to your ideas, rather than to your organization of them.

Research Reports

Any research effort in the government is affected by the politics of the situation. You should not ignore political considerations, but you should take pains to conduct your research objectively and separately from politics. Research is a professional activity and should be kept professional. If you get personally involved in the outcome of a research project, you'll find research in the government terribly frustrating.

Judson Monroe offers the following guidelines for those who do government research and report writing:[4]

- Make sure your data are "clean," that they can stand up to close scrutiny. Present and stand behind your data, but don't try to stretch the facts.

- Expect disagreement over your conclusions. Give others credit for the integrity of their opinions; in return, expect the same credit. Never take criticism personally.

- Make sure you know the politics of a situation before you go out and try to collect data about it. Knowing what sort of political views you're going to run into will help you keep opinions separated from fact.

- Don't start drawing conclusions until you've obtained all the data you need—and all the data you set out to collect.

- Stay out of office politics. Don't get involved in any of the backstabbing and gossip that goes on. This general good advice is especially critical to a researcher.

- When you get into your analysis of results, give at least brief coverage of all sides of any political argument.

- Whenever possible, leave decisions to those with the broadest possible point of view. Explain the options open to the decision makers, explain your point of view, and then leave major decisions to those with the overview.[4]

Monroe gives the following advice to managers and staff for each phase of the research/report-writing process:

Phase	Manager	Staff
Brainstorming, designing the research, and outlining	Tell the researchers and writers everything you can about the nature of the assignment, audience, and subject. Make sure they understand the assignment. Use contract process for the assignment. To maintain focus of the report, write the title for staff.	Make sure you thoroughly understand the assignment. Brainstorm first, then collect data. Brainstorm first, then narrow the scope of the assignment.
Planning research and collecting data	To save money on research, help staff identify sources of existing data. Post lists of existing data. Require evaluation of alternative data sources. Include time and money for a data source search.	To help plan your statistical analysis, use data shells (graphs and charts) without the numbers filled in. Try to locate sources of existing data by talking to people in your agency, etc.

Phase	Manager	Staff
Analyzing results	Help staff keep the study in perspective. Assign at least one generalist to the research team. Be sure you budget staff time for interpretation of data.	Try to find someone outside the research team to help you maintain a broad perspective. Consider the search for causes and recommendations a major part of the research effort.
Assembling the final report	Encourage staff to prepare complete outlines. *The manager is responsible for review and the consequences of the review process.* If you want staff to do a professional job of getting the information you need to make decisions, you need to do a professional job of review.	Build paragraphs by starting with simple headline (topic) sentences, then add details, one sentence at a time in the correct order. Review your own work carefully, using the standards you think management will use. Note potential problems and ask about them. To help ensure a quality report, seek and accept criticism from management.

Example of a How to Plan a Research Project

The county council is running short of funds and is looking for ways to cut costs. Two measures have been proposed and you have been asked to look into them:

1. The council is looking at the special reduced fees for senior citizens at two local golf courses. Should the county continue to give seniors this special rate?

2. The county libraries are open on Sunday afternoons. Should the county continue to keep the libraries open on Sundays?

For item number one, you would need to know:

- How many senior citizens use the courses

- How many take advantage of the reduced fee

- How much revenue is lost because of the reduced fee

- How many would stop using the course if the fees increased

- How many feel that a fee increase would be fair

- How many would be willing to pay extra on a voluntary basis

- What related programs could be changed to help make up the revenue how being lost.

Data Sources for Government Research
Internal (in-house) *sources*

- Management information systems

- Personnel files, especially reports

- Budgets

- Expense records

- Travel records

- Time sheets

- Correspondence files

- Retirement, insurance, and Social Security records

- Minutes of meetings

- Intranet information

External sources include:

- Reports by other local, state, and federal agencies

- Reports from industry, trade journals, and corporate yearly statements

- Reports and files of community service organizations, such as the Chamber of Commerce, charity organizations, unions, fraternal organizations, foundations, and political parties

- Newspaper and magazine files (paper or online)

- University and college faculty studies

- Libraries

- Public records of marriage, health, parentage, age, welfare, place of business, property ownership and use, and taxation

- Census Bureau records

- Sales and inventory records

- Internet sites

Conducting the Research
Collect and document information carefully during the research stage. Make sure that you:

- Distinguish your summarizing from direct quotation.

- Include exact wording of direct quotations.

- Label the exact citation of the source (title, author, etc.).

- Carefully transfer information from notes to draft. Circle quotation marks to make it obvious what is quoted.

- Use the right citation system.

Feasibility Reports

A feasibility report explores the chances of success for a particular project, venture, or commitment. *While a proposal usually recommends one solution, the feasibility report evaluates two or more possible solutions.* The subject of such a report might be a move, the development of a new product or service, an expansion, or a major purchase. The feasibility report examines and compares alternatives, analyzes the pros and cons, and suggests which, if any, of the alternatives are feasible. It includes the following information:

- *A statement of purpose.* This is presented in the introduction to the report. For example, "The purpose of this report is to determine what type and how many new copiers the Training Office should purchase."

- *The problem.* This section gives background information on the problems or events leading up to the reports. For example, a feasibility report on new copiers would describe the wasted time and repair costs involved with the current copiers.

- *The scope.* The scope includes alternatives for accomplishing the purpose and the criteria by which each alternative will be examined, such as cost, personnel required, and legal or other special requirements. For example, the report on new copiers would give a list of the copiers under consideration, and discuss criteria (including the task, time, space, and cost requirements).

- *The alternatives under consideration.* This section gives a detailed evaluation of all alternatives under consideration. Normally, the evaluation of the pros and cons of each alternative (such as each type of copier) makes up a separate section of the report.

- *The conclusion.* The conclusion interprets and summarizes the evaluation of each alternative, usually in the order in which they are discussed in the body of the report.

- *The recommendation(s).* This section states the alternative that best meets the criteria according to the evaluation. For example: "Based on this evaluation, I recommend that we buy the XYZ copier for the Training Office."

Progress Reports

Progress reports, also known as status or activity reports, provide information about ongoing technical work and projects. Topics may include construction, expansion, or research and development. Progress reports are designed to keep management and clients informed about work in progress.

Because progress reports offer updated information on a topic with which the reader should already be familiar, the writer need not include statements of purpose, background, conclusions, and recommendations. Progress reports can be in the form of a memo report or a letter. Regardless of format, they usually include the following information:

- Current projects

- Current problems

- Plans for the next period

- Staffing levels (current and required).

Sample Progress Report

To: John Rey, Comptroller
From: Linda James, Office Manager
Subject: Reorganization of the Filing System

As you requested in your October 12 memo, I have completed plans for reorganizing and centralizing our filing system.

We will start work immediately, with Hollis White and Sandy Melendez supervising.

Our principal objectives will be to:
- Establish a central filing department (with supplementary files where needed)
- Form an efficient messenger service to facilitate the flow of paper to and from the files
- Establish a sound and workable retention and disposition program for all records, reports, orders, and correspondence.

We are convinced that these procedures will save us both time and money by creating a highly efficient, smooth-flowing system.

I have notified department heads of this project and have asked them to assist us in the work that affects their departments. To keep the cost to a minimum and yet complete this work within the next five weeks, priority will be given to requests of those responsible for the success of this project.

I will submit a progress report to you at the end of the second week.

Laboratory Reports

A laboratory report communicates information obtained from a laboratory test or investigation and is longer and more formal than a test report. Laboratory reports state:

- The reason for the investigation

- The conditions, equipment, and procedures for testing

- Any problems encountered

- Conclusions reached

- Recommendations based on the conclusions.

Each laboratory usually establishes the organization of its reports. The laboratory reports often emphasize equipment and procedures because these factors can be critical in determining the accuracy of the data.

Sample Laboratory Report[5]

LABORATORY REPORT
BOREHOLE FOSSIL SAMPLES
BRAINTREE CREEK SITE, WV

INTRODUCTORY SUMMARY

Last week you sent us six fossil samples from the Braintree Creek site. Having analyzed the samples in our lab, we believe they suggest the presence of coal-bearing rock. As you requested, this report will give a summary of the materials and procedures we used in this project, along with any problems we had.

As you know, our methodology is to identify microfossils in the samples, estimate the age of the rock by when the microfossils existed, and then make assumptions about whether the surrounding rock might contain coal.

LAB MATERIALS

Our lab analysis relies on only one piece of specialized equipment: a Piketon electron microscope. Besides the Piketon, we use a simple 400-power manual microscope. Other equipment is similar to that included in any basic geology lab, such as filtering screens and burners.

LAB PROCEDURE

Once we receive a sample, we first try to identify the kinds of microfossils the rocks contain. Our specific lab procedure for your samples consisted of two steps:

Step 1

We used a 400-power microscope to visually classify the microfossils that were present. Upon inspection of the samples, we concluded that there were two main types of microfossils: nannoplankton and foraminifera.

Step 2

Next, we had to extract the microfossils from the core samples you provided. We used two different techniques:
Nannoplankton Extraction Technique
- Selected a pebble-sized piece of the sample
- Thoroughly crushed the piece under water
- Used a dropper to remove some of the material that floats to the surface (It contains the nannoplankton)

- Dried the nannoplankton-water combination
- Placed the nannoplankton on a slide

Foraminifera Extraction Technique

- Boiled a small portion of the sample
- Used a microscreen to remove clay and other un-wanted material
- Dried the remaining material (foraminifera)
- Placed foraminifera on a slide

PROBLEMS ENCOUNTERED

The entire lab procedure went as planned. The only problem was minor and occurred when we removed one of the samples from its shipping container. As the bag was taken from the shipping box, it broke open. The sample shattered when it fell onto the table. Fortunately, we had an extra sample from the same location.

CONCLUSION

Judging from the types of fossils present in the sample, we believe they come from rocks of an age that might contain coal. This conclusion is based on limited testing; so we suggest that you test more samples at the site. We would be glad to help with additional sampling and testing.

I will call you this week to discuss our study and any possibility of follow-up you may wish us to do.

Sincerely,
Joseph Rappaport, Senior Geologist

Test Reports

Test reports are informal, and usually internal, reports on specific tests. They may report the results of a test, or a problem encountered with a test. They may take the format of a memo report or letter, depending on whether the intended reader is internal or external to the organization. Typically, test reports include the following information:

- The test's purpose

- Problems with the test (if applicable)

- Conditions and procedures for testing (if such information is of use or interest to the reader)

- Results and, sometimes, the significance of the results

- Conclusions

- Recommendations.

Trip Reports

Trip reports discuss the accomplishments and findings of an employee's business trip. They establish a permanent record from which other employees can learn. As internal reports, they generally take the memo report format. They contain the following information:

- Purpose of the trip

- Major events

- Conclusions

- Actions taken

- Recommendations.

Trouble Reports

Trouble reports deal with incidents that interfere with normal activity, such as accidents, equipment failures, communication breakdowns, unplanned work stoppages, and damage from fire, flood, or storms. Typically, trouble reports use a memo format, and contain the following information:

- Description of the problem (who, what, when, where, why, and how)

- Resulting injuries or deaths

- Resulting damage

- Costs (in terms of lost work, equipment damage, worker's compensation awards, or lawsuits)

- Witnesses

- Any action taken (including treatment of injuries)

- Recommendations (such as training, equipment improvements, protective clothing, and so on).

Because trouble reports may be used as evidence in lawsuits, it is important to:

- Include precise times, dates, locations, treatment of injuries, names of witnesses, and any other crucial information

- Avoid making statements of condemnation or blame

- Avoid making definite statements about the cause.

Trouble reports enable managers to determine the cause of a problem and make the changes necessary to prevent its recurrence.

Proposals

A proposal is a document that attempts to persuade the reader to follow a plan or course of action. Though a proposal can be internal or external, government proposals are almost always internal.

Internal Proposals

An internal proposal is a document written for others within an organization that suggests a change or improvement. Quite often, such proposals seek approval for a capital expenditure; therefore, persuasion is a primary purpose of these documents.

Typically, internal proposals take the memo report format, and contain the following information:

- Background leading to the problem

- Proposal for fixing the problem

- Specific information about the solution (including cost breakdown; required equipment, personnel, and materials; and a proposed schedule)

- Conclusion that restates recommendations and offers other information or assistance.

Sample Internal Proposal

As you requested, I have evaluated our present accounting system. I recommend we upgrade our software in accordance with the attached specifications. This upgrade will (1) save time, and (2) reduce errors. As soon as I receive your approval, I will contact DataHelp and set up a schedule for the modifications.

Time Savings

The proposed upgrade will reduce the time required to do monthly reconciliations by 35%. In addition, we will be able to prepare quarterly reports in an average of 4 hours as opposed to the 8 hours usually required now.

Reduction in Errors

Our quarterly reports will be more accurate because the software modifications will eliminate much of the manual entry of data we now perform. The modifications also will provide additional cross-checking to further reduce errors.

Because of the time savings and reduction in errors, we should immediately implement this upgrade.[6]

External Proposals

An external proposal is written for a reader outside the writer's organization. An example of an external proposal is a response to a Request For Proposals (RFP) issued by an organization seeking new equipment or services.

The format for external proposals is usually very structured and formal. Public grants usually require full proposals that range from 15 to 100 pages and contain such sections as a cover letter, title page, abstract, introduction, need/problem, objectives, methods, evaluation, dissemination, budget, and appendices.

Minutes of Meetings

As the official record of meetings, minutes must be accurate, complete and clear. They should be taken by someone who is not responsible for either running or facilitating the meeting.

The Importance of Minutes
Minutes:

- Provide a written record—evidence that the meeting took place and addressed issues, actions, and decisions

- Are a reminder and a useful follow-up tool for actions and decisions

- Provide an efficient way to prepare the agenda for the next meeting

- Inform those who did not attend the meeting about what occurred.

Once they are approved, minutes can even serve as evidence in a court of law.

Guidelines for Writing and Distributing Minutes
The following are some useful guidelines for writing and distributing minutes:

1. If you have a well-written agenda, use it as a guide.

2. Use headlines and a consistent format. Examples of headlines are: Date, Objectives, Attendees, Topics, Decisions, Action Items.

3. Include only a summary of the discussion, highlighting the major points. Give people credit for their ideas without inserting opinion or judgmental comments.

4. Provide relevant, specific details on the important topics.

5. Provide complete names and titles.

6. Highlight action items, persons responsible, and deadlines. Then attendees will understand their commitments.

7. Complete and distribute draft minutes as soon as possible. Every day that goes by without minutes, you risk "memory loss."

8. If there are significant disputes about information contained in the minutes, try to resolve the concerns with key participants and, if necessary, issue revised minutes.

9. Issue final versions of the minutes to all meeting attendees (with copies to appropriate files).

What Minutes Typically Include

Minutes typically include:

- Agenda

- Main objectives

- Critical discussion points

- Overheads or data presented

- Agreements and disagreements

- Decisions

- Recommendations

- Issues for further discussion

- Action items (with timeline and persons responsible for each action item).

Example of Meeting Minutes

MEETING MINUTES

DATE: March 24, 2000

FROM: Dr. Jody Harris

TO: Dr. Erica Baldwin, Dr. Valerie Brook, Dr. Kim Chin, Mr. William Cohen, Mr. William Johnston, Dr. James Lee, Dr. Juan Mesa, Dr. Anne Phillips, Ms. Susan Powell, Dr. Derek Smith, Ms. Jonique Thompson,

SUBJECT: Minutes of Type B Meeting with Beta Biologics

Meeting Date: March 22, 2000

Location: Conference Room 4, Building A

Meeting Requestor/Sponsor: Beta Biologics

Type of Meeting: Type B

FDA Meeting Leader: Dr. Juan Mesa

Recorder: Dr. Jody Harris

FDA Attendees: Dr. Derek Smith, Dr. Anne Phillips, Dr. Juan Mesa, Mr. William Johnston, Dr. Valerie Brook, Dr. Jody Harris

Sponsor Attendees: Mr. William Cohen, Dr. Erica Baldwin, Ms. Jonique Thompson, Dr. James Lee

Meeting Objectives:

1. Comparison of the two interpretations of toxicity reports and resolution of differences.

2. Discussion of whether to grant a request that the FDA allow a pharmacokinetic study for Beta Biologic's product to begin in normal, healthy volunteers.

3. Clarification of the FDA's requirements for demonstrating comparability between the old and the new product.

Discussion Points:

- Differences in toxicity reports: how they occurred and which report is reliable.

- Pros and cons of allowing a pharmacokinetic study for Beta Biologic's product to begin in normal, healthy volunteers.

- Requirements for demonstrating comparability between the old and the new product.

Decisions/Agreements Reached:

- The December 1999 toxicity report is not valid because of statistical error. The calculations of toxin levels were incorrect and reflected lower levels than actually occurred.

- Beta must recalculate toxin levels and submit the results.

- The FDA will allow a pharmacokinetic study for Beta Biologic's product to begin in normal, healthy volunteers.

Page 3

- It was decided that, subject to approval by the Dr. Smith, the new biologic must be tested under the following conditions:

  —Subjects must be between the ages of 18 and 45.

  —Each subject must receive a thorough medical examination before being allowed into the program.

Issues Requiring Further Discussion: How to prevent statistical error in the future.

Action Items: Dr. Harris will check with Dr. Smith (Division Director) by March 25 for final approval of the conditions for testing. Dr. Harris will notify Dr. Baldwin of the Division Director's decision.

Attachments/Handouts: November 1999 and December 1999 toxicity reports.

TEST YOURSELF: THE REPORT'S TONE

Rewrite the following report to give it a more personal tone and make it more interesting to read.

Bennett County Hospital
Preliminary Report 2
June 16, 2000

Submitted to
The Board of Trustees
by
The Review Committee

This report is the second in a series of three which the Board of Trustees has requested for its study of feasibility of the proposed expansion of the Bennett County Hospital facilities. The third report of this committee will be submitted in three months' time and will contain the data requested in the Board's letter of December 2, 1999.

General Information

The Bennett County Hospital has received full accreditation from the highest national authority on hospital accreditation, the Joint Commission on Accreditation of Hospitals—the first time that such accreditation has been granted by the Commission.

It can be concluded that this full accreditation is a result of the fact that the hospital meets or exceeds high professional standards in terms of its personnel as well as its physical plant and special services.

This committee ascertained that certain steps had been taken in the past year that have enhanced the hospital's quality of service provided. Intensive care facilities were significantly upgraded. Following completion of a comparative study, nurses' salaries were increased in order to maintain a well-qualified nursing staff. Furthermore, it has been the decision of the hospital to institute the holding of monthly meetings through which the cooperation of staff, administration, and trustees can be maintained ...

A suggested answer can be found in the Appendix, page 318.

A report is an impartial, objective, planned presentation of facts. It should be logical, accurate, reliable, and easy to read. Though generally not as conversational as a letter, a report should nonetheless be friendly and professional.

The three parts of an informal report are the opening, unfolding, and conclusion. A formal report additionally may include an executive summary, table of contents, and appendices.

Following a set format for a business report—whether informal or formal—helps the reader to identify your purpose early on and pay attention to your ideas, rather than your organization of them. Each type of report has a specific purpose. Research reports must be kept separate from politics and should present all sides of an argument. Internal proposals are documents written for others within an organization that suggest a change or improvement; external proposals are written for readers outside the writer's organization. While a proposal usually recommends one solution, a feasibility report generally evaluates two or more possible solutions.

Progress reports, laboratory reports, test reports, trip reports, and trouble reports are all common in the workplace. Each conveys specific information relevant to a project or function.

Finally, the minutes of a meeting constitute an official record of proceedings and therefore must be accurate, complete, and clear.

[1]Pfeiffer, William S. *Pocket Guide to Technical Writing.* Upper Saddle River, NJ: Prentice Hall, 1998, p. 152. Used with permission.

[2]*Writing User-Friendly Documents.* <www.plainlanguage.gov/> 1998.

[3]Spence, Padraic. *Write Smart: The Complete Guide to Business Writing.* Great Barrington, MA, North River Press, 1996, p. 27.

[4]Monroe, Judson. *Effective Research and Report Writing in Government.* New York: McGraw-Hill, 1980, pp. 6-7.

[5]Pfeiffer, William S. *Pocket Guide to Technical Writing.* Upper Saddle River, NJ: Prentice Hall, 1998, pp. 137-138. Used with permission.

[6]Adapted form Spence, Padraic. *Write Smart: The Complete Guide to Business Writing.* Great Barrington, MA: Water Street Press, 1996, p. 32. Used with permission.

CHAPTER 11

Achieving Skill in Technical Writing

Technically Speaking . . . .

"How's the technical writing class going?" Jane asked Tom during his break.

"OK. Our assignment for next class is to write some information for a safety manual. I'm not sure how to do this, but I've noticed one from Centers for Disease Control. It seems very clear, so I may model mine after this one. Here's a description of respiratory protection equipment, for example. "

D. Respiratory Protection

Respiratory hazards may occur through exposure to harmful dusts, fogs, fumes, mists, gases, smoke, sprays, and vapors. The best means of protecting personnel is through the use of engineering controls, e.g., local exhaust ventilation. Only when engineering controls are not practical or applicable shall respiratory protective equipment be employed to reduce personnel exposure.

The Office of Health and Safety is responsible for the Respiratory Protection Program at CDC. Workers requiring the use of respirators must first obtain medical approval from the Occupational Health Clinic physician to wear a respirator before a respirator can be issued. The Industrial Hygiene Section conducts respirator training and fit tests and is responsible for determining the proper type of respiratory protection required for the particular hazard.

Adherence to the following guidelines will help ensure the proper and safe use of respiratory equipment:

Wear only the respirator you have been instructed to use. For example, do not wear a self-containing breathing apparatus if you have been assigned and fitted for a half-mask respirator.

Wear the correct respirator for the particular hazard. For example, some situations, such as chemical spills or other emergencies, may require a higher level of protection than your respirator can handle. Also, the proper cartridge must be matched to the hazard. (A cartridge designed for dusts and mists will not provide protection for chemical vapors.)

Check the respirator for a good fit before each use. Positive and negative fit checks should be conducted.

Check the respirator for deterioration before and after use. Do not use a defective respirator.

Recognize indications that cartridges and canisters are at their end of service. If in doubt, change the cartridges or canisters before using the respirator.

Practice moving and working while wearing the respirator so that you can get used to it.

Clean the respirator after each use, thoroughly dry it, and place the cleaned respirator in a sealable plastic bag.

Store respirators carefully in a protected location away from excessive heat, light, and chemicals.

"What do you think?" Tom asked.

"It seems very clear. Even someone who's not terribly technical could understand this," said Jane.

"That's the whole idea," he responded.

Technical writing involves writing, editing, and publishing information related to technology, medicine, engineering, science, or a similar field.

We can distinguish technical writing from other types of writing by its:

- Purpose

- Style

- Subject matter

- Criteria.

The *purpose* of technical writing is to inform, instruct, describe, explain, or otherwise document scientific or industrial processes and mechanisms.[1]

Because the primary purpose of technical and business writing is to convey information accurately, the *style* of business and technical writing is utilitarian. The writer is not concerned with painting word pictures or dazzling the reader with new and daring visions. The focus is on the information. The technical writer aims to convey information as clearly, completely, and concisely as possible.

Technical writers deal with specific, factual *subject matter* related to engineering, computers and other technology, and physical, biological, and social sciences. Technical writing is concerned with objects, processes, systems, or abstract ideas. The focus is on describing and explaining. The reader should be able to take away knowledge about how something works or how to do something.

According to Gary Blake and Robert W. Bly, technical writing must meet the following *criteria*:

- Accuracy

- Usefulness

- Conciseness

- Completeness

- Clarity

- Consistency

- Correctness

- Appropriateness for the reader

- Organization

- Interest to the reader.[2]

THE AUDIENCE FOR TECHNICAL WRITING

The reader of a technical document might be a technical professional, a non-technical manager, or a general reader.

Technical writing should be targeted to the reader's technical proficiency and understanding. Often, the technical writer is writing for an audience with a diverse background. Some readers may know a great deal about the topic, and may be bored or insulted by writing that spells out what they already know. Other readers who know less about the topic may be confused by complex content. To make your writing appropriate to your audience:

- *Define the audience.* Who will be reading this document? What kind of background and education do they have? What kind of functions do they perform? Why will they be reading this? What terms will they need to have defined? What jargon will they commonly use?

- *Write for the majority, while accommodating minorities.* When writing for a mixed audience of technical and non-technical people, include enough data to satisfy the technical readers, while also describing the data in terms that lay readers can understand. Use the "gist" test—non-technical readers should be able to get the "gist" of your ideas.

- *When the primary audience is non-technical, flesh out explanations.* When introducing new terms, include a separate sentence or paragraph defining them.

- *When the primary audience is technical, include parenthetical explanations.* These serve as quick "refreshers."

- *Put yourself in your readers' place and ask the questions they would ask.* Try asking "Who?" "What?" "Where?" "When?" "Why?" and "How?" A reader assembling a swing set, for example, might ask:

  —What tools do I need?

  —Where should it be placed (grass, sand, acceptable slope)?

  —Who can use it (weight and height restrictions)?

  —How do I assemble it?

Carol M. Barnum and Saul Carliner[3] share the following information about audiences for writers of technical documents:

Readers of Technical Communication

What research tells us about audience	*What technical writers should do*
• People decide how much attention to pay to a document, based on the product, the packaging, and the document's level of difficulty.	• Minimize the amount of reading required. • Consider how readers will use the document and organize and design it accordingly.
• Readers use documents as tools. Sullivan and Flowers discovered that, in using a library manual: — No one carefully read more than two sentences at a time. — Most people began to use the product before they turned to the manual. — People used the manual only when they were not successful in achieving their goal. — Most did not read the introduction first. — Most did not read any section in its entirety.	• Make the table of contents and index match topics people are looking for. • Design pages for easy skimming and scanning. • Use structures such as numbers and lists of steps to help readers.
• Readers actively interpret documents as they read.	• Use active voice and action-verb sentences with people or organizations as subjects of the sentences.

What research tells us about audience	What technical writers should do
• Readers interpret documents in light of their own knowledge and expectations.	• Provide clear organization. • Follow the *given-new contract*: Present information in a framework of what readers already know or have been given. • Maintain coherence and consistency by using: — headings, listings, changes in typography, and page placement to show organization — *chunks*, or small, visually distinct sections of information — hierarchical organization of information (*queuing*). • Provide multiple pathways through a document by using a combination of words and pictures to give information.

TECHNICAL DEFINITIONS

In technical writing it is important to specify meaning. A word or phrase can mean one thing in everyday speech, and quite another when it relates to technology. For example, a "chord" is a combination of tones sounded at the same time, but it is also a straight line joining two points on a curve. The technical writer must understand the correct meaning for the technology, and make sure the reader does as well.

Technical definitions can be classified into three categories:

- Informal or parenthetical

- Formal

- Extended.

Informal or Parenthetical Definitions

An informal definition explains a term by giving a familiar word or phrase as a synonym. For example:

"This is a discrete, or distinct, step in the process."

Sometimes, informal definitions are included in parentheses immediately after the word they define. For example:

"This process includes 10 discrete (distinct and separate) steps."

Formal Definitions

Formal definitions are generally one to three sentences. A formal definition should include the following:

- The term

- The category in which the term is classified

- Unique features of the term compared with other terms or elements in the category.

For example:

"A mastiff [term] is a large dog [category] with a short fawn-colored coat [distinguishing features]."

Extended Definitions

For more complex terms or terms with a very specific meaning, a technical writer might extend the definition through:

- Example

- Analogy

- Analysis.

Example

Using specific examples gives the reader details useful in forming a mental picture. For example:

> "A diphthong is a single speech sound that begins with one vowel sound and moves to another in the same syllable, such as 'oi' in 'coil.'"

Analogy

Using an analogy involves noting a correspondence between two otherwise unlike things. For example:

> "A disk pack is a computer storage device consisting of several magnetic disks that can be used and stored as a unit. Like a jukebox, it sorts the stored disks, allowing the operator to choose the disk containing the desired information."

Analysis

The following table summarizes techniques for analyzing definitions.

Technique	Example
explaining the term's causes	Malaria is an infectious disease marked by cycles of chills, fever, and sweating. It is associated with humid, tropical climates because it is transmitted by the bite of the female anopheles mosquito.

Technique	Example
breaking down the definition into component parts, with a definition of each component part	"Fire is the visible heat energy released from the rapid oxidation of a fuel. . . . the elements necessary to create fire (are) oxygen, heat, and burnable material or fuel. Air provides sufficient oxygen for combustion; the intensity of the heat needed to start a fire depends on the characteristics of the burnable material or fuel. A burnable substance is one that will sustain combustion after an initial application of heat to start it."
explaining the term's origins	"Dismal," which means gloomy or depressing, comes from the Latin *dies mali* ("evil days").
making a negative comparison of the item with an unlike item (only if the reader will be familiar with the unlike item)	Pizzicato means to play by plucking, not by using a bow. (We assume that the reader knows what a bow is.)

Rules For Definitions

The following table summarizes some techniques for writing clear definitions.

Rule	Instead of:	Try:
State definitions positively.	"A condition that is endemic is not rare."	"An endemic condition is widespread in a particular area or people."
Avoid defining a term by restating it.	"Iridescence occurs when an object becomes iridescent."	"Iridescence is a state where objects produce an array of rainbow-like colors."

Rule	Instead of:	Try:
Avoid "is when" and "is where." (These definitions do not include a category.) Instead, tell "is what."	"An ion is when an atom acquires a net electric charge."	"An ion is an atom, group of atoms, or molecule that has acquired a net electric charge."
Avoid or explain terms unfamiliar to your readers.	"Pizzicato means plucking with the fingers instead of using a bow."	"Pizzicato means playing a stringed instrument, such as a violin, by plucking the strings instead of drawing a bow across them."

TECHNICAL DESCRIPTIONS

James H. Shelton identifies two basic types of technical descriptions:

- Mechanism descriptions

- Process descriptions.[4]

Mechanism Description

To develop a mechanism description:

- Explain the mechanism's purpose and general operating standards.

  —What is the mechanism's main use?

  —Where is the mechanism used?

—How often does the mechanism operate, and for how long?

—What conditions must be met before the mechanism can be operated? (For example, some mechanisms work only at certain temperature or humidity levels.)

—To what extent do people control the mechanism, directly or indirectly?

- Visually describe the mechanism as a whole.

    —Give its general size and dimensions.

    —Compare its shape to related mechanisms.

- Describe the principles of the mechanism's operation.

    —How does the mechanism work?

    —What are the major components? (Note the number of features and the relative size of each.)

- List and describe all parts of the mechanism.

    —List each specific part.

    —Explain how each part functions in relation to other parts.

    —Explain where each part is located.

    —Explain how each part functions.

TEST YOURSELF: WRITING A MECHANISM DESCRIPTION

Using the guidelines above, write a description of a computer mouse.

Example given on page 319.

Process Description

To write a process description:

- Explain the process's purpose and general operating standards.

  —Why is the process performed? What is its primary function?

  —Who performs the process?

  —Where does the process occur?

  —How often does the process occur?

  —How long does the process take?

  —What conditions must be met before the process can be performed?

- Describe the process as a whole.

  —List the major divisions in the process. (Major divisions in washing a car might include wetting, soaping, rinsing, drying, and waxing.)

  —List all necessary materials.

  —Describe special skills needed to perform the process.

- Describe each step in the process.

    —List all steps in the process. (Steps in washing a car might include wetting the car, mixing soap with water, applying soapy water to the car, scrubbing, rinsing, drying with soft towels, applying wax, and buffing.)

    —Describe when and where each step occurs.

    —Describe how long each step takes.

The following is an example of a process description from Microsoft Word:

Select text and graphics by using the mouse

To select	Do this
Any amount of text	Drag over the text.
A word	Double-click the word.
A graphic	Click the graphic.
A line of text	Move the pointer to the left of the line until it changes to a right-pointing arrow, and then click.
A paragraph	Move the pointer to the left of the paragraph until it changes to a right-pointing arrow, and then double-click. Or triple-click anywhere in the paragraph.

TECHNICAL INSTRUCTIONS

Most of us have had the experience of trying unsuccess-fully to follow directions. Maryann Piotrowskil says this:

> Though seemingly a simple task, writing clear instruc-tions demands careful thought and execution. Every step must be delineated, every doubt clarified, every risk de-fined. Whether a set of directions is a formal document that will be included in a procedures manual or an infor-mal note explaining how to get to the new plant, it should be simple and clear.[5]

Like technical descriptions, technical instructions help the reader understand how a process or mechanism works. Technical instructions must also show the reader how he or she can perform a process. Typical processes for which in-structions are required include:

- Operating

- Maintaining

- Repairing

- Assembling

- Testing.

To write technical instructions:

1. State the purpose of the instructions.

2. List the conditions that must be met prior to beginning the operation (such as equipment and skills require-ments, climate conditions, and time restraints).

3. Give the sequence of instructions.

Tips for making instructions easier to understand include:

- Divide the process into short, simple steps.

- Use familiar terms. Don't frustrate your reader. Use language everyone can understand.

- Label all steps with numbers or with words indicating sequence (such as "first," "second," "next," "then")

- Adhere strictly to chronological order. Present instructions in the order in which they are to be performed.

- If two operations must be performed simultaneously, be sure to make this clear:

  Example: "While holding the Control key, press the F4 key."

- When an early step is going to have an effect on a later step, say so.

- Be concise, but do not confuse the reader by leaving out too many articles ("a," "an," and "the") or explanatory phrases.

- Consider including an illustration labeling the parts named in the instructions.

- Move from the familiar to the unfamiliar. Relate what the readers don't know to what they do know.

- Reassure the reader. Insert occasional phrases that tell readers when they are proceeding correctly. (For example, "If you have completed this step properly, the green light will flash when you push the red button.")

- Give all necessary warnings. Explain all conditions under which an operation should or should not be performed. (For example, "CAUTION: Do not operate the equipment during electrical storms.")

- Explain the reasons for performing a step. This will help readers understand the process and complete the step correctly.

- Use an easy-to-follow format. Number the steps so that the reader can focus on one step at a time and find the next step easily.

- Include visual aids. Use simple drawings or diagrams to explain a process or mechanism more clearly than words. Make sure the visual aids are simple and clearly labeled.

- Test the instructions. Have someone unfamiliar with the process follow the instructions so you can determine where they are confusing or unclear. Revise any problem areas and re-test your instructions.[6]

Lists are often used when writing technical instructions. Lists are effective for:

- Presenting information that is parallel

- Reducing the confusion that can occur when a series of items is presented in paragraph format.

Example: Changing a Paragraph to a List

The Word 97 menu bar includes menus for File, for creating, opening, and closing files; Edit, for cutting, copying, pasting, finding, replacing, and replacing text; View, for changing the view and the display of items such as toolbars and rulers; Insert, for adding new objects such as footnotes, pictures, and linked objects; Format, for changing format options such as font and paragraph format; Tools, for using specialized functions such as spellcheck, grammar check, and hyphenation; Table, for creating and formatting tables; Window, for arranging the display of documents; and Help, for accessing the online help system.

Here is a better alternative:

The Word 97 menu bar includes the following menus:

- File—for creating, opening, and closing files

- Edit—for cutting, copying, pasting, finding, replacing, and replacing text

- View—for changing the view and the display of items such as toolbars and rulers

- Insert—for adding new objects such as footnotes, pictures, and linked objects

- Format—for changing format options such as font and paragraph format

- Tools—for creating and formatting tables

- Window—for arranging the display of documents

- Help—for accessing the online help system.

FORMS OF TECHNICAL WRITING

Many of the types of reports described previously are used for technical writing, including feasibility reports, status/ progress reports, test reports, trip reports, trouble reports, technical formal reports, and technical proposals. In addition, technical writing is used in developing:

- Playscripts

- Technical manuals

- Journal articles

- Specifications

- Help systems.

Playscripts

A playscript is a format in which the writer identifies not only all the actions in a task, but all those who play a role in performing the task. Playscripts are useful for helping the reader know what to expect next. For example, a playscript might use one role to identify a computer user's input, and another role to describe the computer's expected response.

Example: Creating a New Letter Using the Elegant Letter Template in Word 97

User: Use the mouse to click on the File menu.
Computer: The File drop-down menu appears.

User: Use the mouse to click the New option.
Computer: The New dialog box appears.

User: In the New dialog box, click on the Letters & Faxes folder.
Computer: The dialog box displays icons for each of the templates available under the Letters & Faxes folder.

User:	Click on the ElegantLetter.dot icon.
Computer:	The icon is highlighted.
User:	Click on the OK button.
Computer:	A new document window opens. The window includes placeholders for the organization's letterhead, the recipient's address, the salutation, the body, and the closing.

If the writer were using this playscript to develop a procedure, the names of the "players" would be eliminated, and
the computer's "role" would be presented in a special format, such as italics, after each step. For example:

1. Us the mouse to click on the File menu.
   The File drop-down menu appears.

2. Use the mouse to click on the New option.
   The New dialog box appears.

3. In the New dialog box, click on the Letters & Faxes
   folder.
   The dialog box displays icons for each of the templates
   available under the Letters & Faxes folder.

4. Click on the ElegantLetter.doc icon.
   The icon is highlighted.

5. Click on the OK button.
   A new document window opens. The window includes
   placeholders for the organization's letterhead, the
   recipient's address, the salutation, the body, and the
   closing.

Technical Manuals

Technical manuals are documents written to help technical and non-technical readers use and maintain equipment. Common types of manuals include:

- Installation manuals

- Instruction and users' manuals

- Maintenance manuals

- Operations manuals—theoretical information about how equipment operates

- Sales manuals—information about specifying and purchasing equipment.

Operations and users' manuals should be written for a general, non-technical audience. Manuals make extensive use of technical descriptions and instructions. Illustrations, especially labeled diagrams, will help non-technical users locate parts as they are discussed.

Installation and maintenance manuals, on the other hand, are meant primarily for the highly technical expert who installs, repairs, and maintains a piece of equipment. They rely heavily on such tools as schematics and exploded diagrams.

Format for Technical Manuals

Maintenance manuals are generally written for the person who repairs and maintains a piece of equipment. The reader may be highly skilled or semi-skilled. Illustrations might include schematic diagrams, blueprints, tables of operating data, performance curves, and specifications. A general format for maintenance manuals is:

- Title/cover page

- Preface/introduction

- Table of contents

- Mechanism descriptions

- Process descriptions

- User instructions

- Appendices

- Glossary

- Index.

Guidelines for Technical Manuals

Blake and Bly offer general guidelines for writing better manuals:

- Remember that manual writing is instruction writing. Practice by writing instructions for non-technical activities.

- Be complete. It is better to assume too little knowledge, experience, and familiarity with your technology on the part of the reader than to assume too much.

- Be clear and correct.

- Be unambiguous. It is better to be repetitious and perfectly clear than brief and possibly unclear.

- Warnings should be set off from the rest of the text using special typefaces. Critical warnings can be boldfaced and put in boxes, with secondary warnings in italics or underlined.

- Use the imperative voice—"Connect the cables" is better than "The cables should be connected."[7]

Steps in Creating a Manual[8]

The following steps are useful for creating a manual:

1. Prepare a documentation plan.

   Complete an audience analysis by answering these questions:

   - Who will read this document?

   - What do they want?

   - How much do they already know?

   - How (and where, and when) will they use the document?

   - Use your audience analysis—for content, design, layout, and print (e.g., will the audience want wipe-clean pages?).

2. Brainstorm and mind map (see Chapter 2).

3. Complete a task analysis.

   Elements of a task analysis include:

   - The performer—the person completing the task

   - The action—the work in the task (verb and noun)

- The environment—atmosphere and conditions under which the performer must complete the action, including performer's attitude and emotions

- The goal—what the action will achieve

- Requirements—tools, knowledge, or experience the performer must have

- Your assumptions—things you will take for granted (e.g., I assume the reader will know how to turn on the machine).

Steps in completing a task analysis are:

a. Select a task.

b. Divide the task into actions.

c. Define each action's goal.

d. List the action's performer.

e. List the starting conditions (including any previously completed actions).

f. List the requirements.

g. List your assumptions.

h. Describe the environment.

4. Complete an audience-task matrix.

- List all members of your audience on one axis.

- On the other axis, list every task you have analyzed.

- Note which tasks apply to each audience member.

5. Establish formats for layout and writing.

Journal Articles

Publishing an article in a trade or professional journal offers many advantages:

- Demonstrates your expertise to others in your field, enhancing your professional standing

- Provides good publicity for your organization

- Allows you to contribute to the pool of technical knowledge

- Provides an opportunity for you to learn more about the subject on which you are writing.

Although it is prestigious, being published in a journal is not impossible. There are more than 6,000 business, technical, academic, scientific, and trade publications in the United States. These journals are aimed at specialized audiences of professionals with knowledge and experience in a particular field, and journal editors are always interested in concise, well-written, relevant articles. Topics include case studies; trends; new ideas and products; technological advances; improvements in manufacturing techniques; research findings; and experiments.

The key to an effective journal article is clear purpose and good organization. Outlining the article is critical to getting it published. The subject must be in accordance with the journal's specific subject matter, and it must present new and interesting information for its readers.

When you are preparing to write a journal article, follow these steps:

1. *Evaluate the topic.* What new contributions can you make to the field? Why are your ideas worthy of publication?

2. *Evaluate the effort.* What kind of work will be required to research, organize, draft, and edit the article? Is publication worth the time and effort?

3. *Identify relevant journals.* Many journals are published by professional societies and organizations. A little research can help you identify journals that might be interested in your topic.

4. *Research relevant journals.* Once you have narrowed your list to a few possible journals, find out more about each. How many readers does it have? What are those readers' interests? Does it have a good reputation? Are articles from it cited in other works? Does your article relate to the journal's goals?

5. *Determine the journals' requirements.* From your research, you should be able to narrow down your list of journals to one or two. Contact each journal to find out what it requires in terms of style, tone, length, and format. (Many journals provide author's guidelines to prospective authors.) Review some back issues to get a feel for style and content.

6. *Write and submit the article.* Remember, the journal's editors may (and probably will) edit your work. However, they will want to start with a manuscript that conforms to their guidelines, and that is clear, concise, and well-written.

7. *Read it and reap the rewards of authorship.*

Specifications

A specification (or "spec") is a detailed statement of work. Specifications often describe materials, dimensions, and workmanship for building, installation, or manufacturing projects. Because unclear specifications can be costly in terms of delays and potential lawsuits, it is crucial that specifications be:

- Carefully researched

- Accurately written

- Carefully revised.

The government requires agencies to write specifications when contracting for equipment or services. The specifications define exactly what the contractor is to provide: a technical description of the device; estimated cost; estimated delivery date; and standards for design, manufacture, workmanship, testing, training, governing codes, inspection, and delivery. Government specifications must comply with particular rules and formats, and government agencies publish guidelines on writing them.

Steps in developing specifications include:[10]

1. Get a statement of the problem and requirements.

2. Analyze and classify the problem and requirements.

3. Restate this requirements specification in your words to the contractor.

4. Begin your design specification process.

When writing specifications:

- Write clearly

- Use appropriate technical language

- Be precise

- Be concise

- Be complete

- Use the present tense—Not, "The equipment *will have* (or *must have* or *should have*) six components," but "The equipment *has* six components."

Help Systems

The first step in developing a help system is to examine the reader's needs. What will the reader want to know? What terms need to be defined? What questions might the reader ask? What procedures will the reader want to perform?

One of the technical writer's primary concerns must be retrievability—the ability of readers to locate specific information in the document quickly and easily. To aid users of printed documents, writers often rely on several types of help devices:

- *Table of contents*—a listing of all topics in the document, divided into broad sections like the chapters in a book, with page numbers

- *"How do I?" index*—an index of common tasks that users might perform, and the number of the page where the task is explained

- *Alphabetical index*—an index that lists all topics in the document and their page numbers, sorted alphabetically by topic title or keyword

- *Thematic index*—an index that lists all topics in the document, with topics grouped by category (e.g., "drawing objects," "fields," "file formats")

- *Glossary*—a list of definitions of terms or acronyms that may be unfamiliar to readers

- *References section*—a list of outside sources of more information.

For an online help system, the technical writer will also write a series of topics that explains common tasks and defines terms. These topics are then organized into many different types of devices, some of which are similar to those used in a printed document. Such devices include:

- *Table of contents*—a listing of all topics in the help system, divided into broad sections like the chapters in a book

- *Thematic index*—an index that lists all topics in the help text, with topics grouped by category (e.g., "drawing objects," "fields," "file formats")

- *Glossary*—a list of terms that may be unfamiliar to readers

- *Alphabetical index*—an index that lists all topics in the help text, sorted alphabetically by topic title or keyword

- *"How do I?" index*—an index of common tasks that users might perform.

The difference between these online devices and their printed counterparts is the way the reader accesses the information. Instead of turning to a page, the reader might click on a hypertext link that jumps to and opens the online page that discusses the topic.

Online help systems also allow the inclusion of other devices:

- *Pop-up boxes*—boxes that "pop up" on the screen when the user clicks on or places the cursor above specified words or phrases (such boxes are often used for short definitions of terms)

- *Coaches, wizards, or assistants*—software programs that lead the user through a process, asking what the user wants and then performing actions based on the answers

- *"Show me" links*—hypertext links that, when clicked on, demonstrate the action the reader wants to perform

- *Hypertext links*—links that, when clicked on, take the reader to a related topic or even to an outside source of more information, such as a Web site.

Common Standards for Online Help Systems

Help systems rely on a set of standards for creating help features such as interactive tables of contents and indexes, links to related topics, and pop-ups. Common standards for online help systems include:

- Windows Help, or WinHelp, a set of standards currently used on many Windows-based programs

- HTML-based help, an emerging set of standards based on the HyperText Markup Language (HTML) used in World Wide Web pages.

A key difference between WinHelp and HTML-based help is the file structure:

- In WinHelp, each topic "page" is saved as a Rich Text Format (RTF) file containing format control codes. A help compiler program compiles those files into hypertext Help files, which the Help engine displays.

- In HTML-based help, each topic "page" is saved as an HTML format file containing HTML codes and other controls. These codes and controls specify how to display the text and how to jump to other topics or even other Web sites.

HTML-based help allows for better display options than WinHelp (for example, displaying simultaneously a table of contents and a selected topic from that table). It also allows for the use of more hypertext links (such as links to related topics within the index, and links to intranet and Internet sites).

Tools for Creating Help Files

The most important tool for creating help files is the technical writer. The writer is responsible for developing a help system that meets the audience's needs. That requires:

- Careful audience analysis

- Clear writing

- Logical organization

- Thoughtful attention to details such as topic headings.

For example, the most sophisticated help system in the world will not help if the topic discusses "landscape printing" and the reader only wants to "print the document on the wide part of the paper."

Because they are text-based, standard HTML documents can be created with any word-processing program. However, the codes and controls used to create help tables of contents and indexes are more complicated. For the "grunt work" of formatting and coding text, a number of software programs are available. Many software programs also allow single-source editing (the creation of one master Help file that can then be converted to different formats such as print or HTML).

Employers often expect technical writers to be familiar with these programs. Many of these programs are available free, if only on a trial basis, and many can be downloaded or ordered from the Internet. Some common authoring tools can be obtained as follows:

Program	Company Web site
RoboHelp	www.blue-sky.com
HelpBreeze	www.solutionsoft.com
Microsoft HTML Help	www.microsoft.com

Technical writing involves writing, editing, or publishing information related to technology, medicine, engineering, or a similar field. It is distinguished from other types of writing by purpose, writing style, subject matter, and criteria.

Technical writing should be targeted to the technical proficiency and understanding of the readers. If you have a mixed audience, include enough data to satisfy the technical readers, while adding explanations where needed to help lay readers. Technical documents should have a minimum of text, clear organization, and a design that allows skimming. A variety of techniques can be used to help readers interpret documents in light of their own knowledge and expectations.

In technical writing, it is important to specify meaning. Technical definitions can be informal, formal, or extended. Technical writers also frequently must describe mechanisms and processes. In doing so, they explain the purpose, describe the mechanism or process as a whole, and then explain each part or step.

It is also important to know how to write clear, easy-to-understand instructions.

Specific forms of technical writing include playscripts, technical manuals, technical journal articles, specs, and help systems.

[1]Shelton, James H. *Handbook for Technical Writing.* Lincolnwood, IL: NTC Publishing Group, 1994.

[2]Blake, Gary and Robert W. Bly. *The Elements of Technical Writing.* New York: Macmillan, 1993.

[3]Carol M. Barnum and Saul Carliner. *Techniques for Technical Communicators.* New York: Macmillan Publishing Co., 1993.

[4]Shelton, James H. *Handbook for Technical Writing.* Lincolnwood, IL: NTC Publishing Group, 1994.

[5]Piotrowski, Maryann V. *Effective Business Writing: A Guide for Those Who Write on the Job.* New York: HarperCollins, 1996, p. 71.

[6]Ibid, pp. 71-72.

[7]Blake, Gary and Robert W. Bly. *The Elements of Technical Writing.* New York: Macmillan, 1993.

[8]Copp, Stephanie. "Principles of Technical Writing." English 210 Technical Writing. <http://itrc.uwaterloo.ca/~engl210e/BookShelf/Required/Manual1/sec_9.htm> (30 July 1998)

[9]Blake, Gary, and Robert W. Bly. *The Elements of Technical Writing.* New York: Macmillan, 1993.

[10]Ibid.

CHAPTER 12

Other Forms of Workplace Writing

Doing Whatever Is Needed

Maria, Lou, Pat, and Fred were a team of writers charged with developing a budget justification statement. Today was the first team meeting.

"I guess we'd better decide who does what," Fred said.

The group decided that Maria and Lou would draft the document, Fred would develop graphics, and Pat and Fred would both edit it.

"Do we know what our main goal is?" Maria asked. "I know we're asking for increased funding for the state school breakfast program, but are we clear on what the increased funding will do for the state?"

"And specifically, how it will affect *people* in the state," added Pat.

Lou spoke up: "You're right. We need to think that through. And we also need to consider our audience—the legislators."

"I guess we have a lot of work ahead," said Fred. "Let's get out our calendars and set some milestones."

Today's writers need to develop a wide array of skills. They must be able to work with others on a team, as well as compose and/or edit a variety of documents.

Employees at all levels are asked to help compose budget justification statements; make outlines for briefings; ghost-write; and help write or revise policies, procedures, and regulations.

COLLABORATIVE WRITING

Most business writing is collaborative writing. You are team-writing any time more than one person must be involved before the document is final. Even if one person writes the first draft on her or his own, it may go through many technical experts, managers, editors, and people savvy about the politics of the issue before it is released. Anyone involved in the writing process must know how to work with others—how to plan, organize, and both give and take suggestions.

Guidelines for Collaborative Writing

The following are some guidelines for collaborative writing:

- All members of the team should understand who will be drafting, who will be editing, and who will be signing off on which sections of the document. Roles, responsibilities, and deadlines should be clarified as early as possible. If team members cannot agree on roles, the delegator may need to make assignments.

- Both delegators and writers need to communicate expectations and feelings. Any problems or frustrations that arise should be discussed and worked out.

- Team members should be certain that they fully understand the purpose, audience, and subject of the document.

- Delegators, writers, and reviewers should coordinate their work. They should develop a production schedule or milestone chart, build in extra time to allow for the unexpected, and make sure the deadlines are realistic for everyone.

- If more than one person is doing the writing, the project should be broken into to manageable chunks and sections assigned accordingly. One of the editor's jobs is to make sure the document sounds as if one person wrote it.

- When several team members are using the same software, they can save time by using software tools:

  — Use the "track changes" feature to strike through or add text in a contrasting color without destroying text.

  — Select a split screen to display the original and the edited version with the changes highlighted.

- Reviewers should make constructive comments. To make the project a learning experience, refrain from editing, but ask questions instead. "Have you included enough details here?" or "Is this headline clear enough?"

How Groups Work

Small groups have lives and personalities of their own. Like individuals, they go through stages of development. Being aware of these stages can help you understand some of the frustrations you may face when you collaborate on a writing project. The most common model of group development involves four stages: forming, storming, norming, and performing:

- *Forming.* In this initial stage, a group of people assembles for a particular purpose, such as writing a proposal or major report. At this point, they are still a collection of individuals who may or may not have worked together before or even known one another.

- *Storming*. Each individual now attempts to fit into the group. Group members raise individual issues and concerns that must be addressed before the group can develop further.

- *Norming*. Now that individual issues are resolved, group members establish standards for the group's behavior and performance. Goals and objectives are set, and group members are assigned roles and tasks.

- *Performing*. The group now functions as a unit, and its members work together productively. The group can now perform the tasks assigned to it and achieve its mission.

A group may go in and out of these stages. Group members may begin to storm, for example, right after a period of productive performing.

GHOSTWRITING

You may be asked to write a letter for someone else's signature or prepare a report or speech for an upper-level manager. On the other hand, you may ask others to do the same for you. Understanding the realities of ghostwriting can help you and your partner complete the project successfully.

Delegating the Task

Delegating work just to get it off your desk can be self-defeating if you are disappointed in the results and end up completing the task yourself.

Make sure you delegate the writing task to someone who understands the situation sufficiently to take on the job, and then make sure that you work closely with the person, especially if the individual has little experience writing. Make sure you are clear about exactly what you want and that you communicate your expectations to the writer.

Do not expect the writer to duplicate your style, but instead, add some of your own personal touches before signing off on it.

Taking on the Task

If you are the one asked to write the letter, speech, or report, make sure your understand the task as thoroughly as possible. Ask questions, become informed, and consider this a learning opportunity. If it is a long document, write one section and get feedback from the person who asked you to write before going on to the rest. You should expect changes to be made, even though the draft represents your best effort.[1]

BUDGET JUSTIFICATIONS

Competition for government resources is fierce and requires rigor in the planning and writing of budget requests. Writing skill could be the competitive edge that makes your budget request succeed next year.

The primary purpose of a written budget is to give friendly legislators the ammunition they need to argue your case and to justify their votes to their constituency. If you are concerned with the federal budget or a state budget, you have several different audiences to which you direct your justification:

- Office of Management and Budget examiners (for a federal budget)

- Agency budget staff

- Congressional or legislative staffers

- Members of Congress or the legislature

- Lobbyists.

Effective budget justifications usually describe events that are intended to occur within a year or more. Their time frame is the end of the budget year (September 30), unless a different time frame is stated. The budget justification describes *intended* outcomes, not *hoped-for* outcomes. These outcomes are within the agency's jurisdiction, program authority, and power.

Before you write, make sure you have reviewed and analyzed the following information:

- Description of agency, legislative authority, and appropriation language.

- For each activity:

  —Statement of functions and purpose

  —Description of changes requested for the budget year as compared to the current year

  —Productivity increase and management improvements

  —Summary of budget approved by the Office of Management and Budget (OMB) or comparable state agency

  —Historical tables:

    —Program costs linked to appropriations

    —Employment by organization unit

    —Obligations or costs by object class

    —Summary of workload indicators.

As you organize the justification information, make sure you include:

- Goals

- Objectives

- Workloads

- Accomplishments

- Beneficiaries served

- Funding needs.

Effective budget justifications are:

- *Meaningful.* They describe significant outcomes that affect people, not agencies or things. If possible, they should relate to people of importance to the audience.

- *Measurable.* They quantify the impact of the intended program on the country. They state the unit of measurement precisely and use verifiable data.

- *Clear.* They use precise names, action verbs, and plain language.

- *Realistic.* They allow for aggressive, achievable goals.

- *Comprehensive.* They explain everything in the best possible light, address their own weakest points, and answer the toughest questions before they are asked.

The justification should show clearly the cause-and-effect relationship between the funding and the achievement of the outcome or objective.

For example, if the objective is a 20% decrease in malnutrition cases, the justification will document the relationship between the level of poverty and the incidence of malnutrition, and describe how requested grant funds will be distributed among the states, local food banks, and non-profit organizations that feed qualified, low-income families.

The budget strategy merges the agency's strategic plan with its political plan. The *strategic plan* addresses the agency's mission, goals, results-oriented objectives, performance measures, and strategies. The *political plan* addresses reasons why members of Congress or the legislature will support the budget.

Using an example of funding for school breakfasts, Phillip Blackerby and Melissa Hield show an effective way to structure a budget justification request:[2]

Sample Budget Justification Request

Paragraph	Purpose	Example
First	• Puts the strongest possible statement in the lead • Invites the reader to read on • Describes the primary result of the request Supporting sentences explain consequences, especially to local constituents	"With full funding, 75,000 children will improve their grades by an average of 109% and increase school attendance by an average of 20%. In the long run, these children will be less likely to drop out of school, commit crimes, or depend on welfare. As a result, future human service programs at all levels of government will have lighter caseloads and smaller funding needs."

Paragraph	Purpose	Example
Second	• Develops logic between results described in first paragraph and agency's actions • Shows how agency's funding leads to achieving results	"Studies show that a good breakfast increases concentration, and free breakfasts at school give pupils an incentive to attend school. Increased concentration and attendance improve grades by an average of 10% for School Breakfast Program participants. The program distributes funds by formulae to state Boards of Education for school district grants in the 100 hungriest counties. District programs work with local food banks to serve nutritious breakfast to qualified grade school children from low income families."
Third and subsequent	• Show how specific changes in the funding level affect program performance described in first two paragraphs. • Address funding levels by object class.	"Requested funding increases the number of children receiving school breakfasts by 9.5% and extends eligibility from 85 of the hungriest counties to 100. This increased performance includes an 8.1% increase in grants and a net 1.4% decrease in administrative overhead. . . ."
Last	• Summarizes • Reinforces and strengthens primary point in first paragraph • Leaves a final and lasting impression on the reader • Should be memorable	"A good day starts with a good breakfast: a good life starts with a good education. Simply feeding hungry children breakfast improves their school performance now and keeps them out of jail and off the welfare rolls later."

BRIEFINGS AND PRESENTATIONS

"Public speaking" may mean presenting your idea to a committee of four co-workers or delivering a presentation to a group of 250 people. In either case, careful preparation and planning are essential.

The outstanding speakers you have heard and envied may have made it look easy. However, their ability to present their ideas effectively took effort. They spent their fair share of time in preparation before they ever got up in front of their audience to speak.

Steps in Preparing

1. Analyze audience, situation, and speaker.

2. Determine goal.

   —Why are you addressing this audience?

   —What specific action do you want to see happen as a result of this presentation?

   —Three months from now, what do you want people to remember?

3. Determine sources of data.

4. Gather information.

5. Determine main points and supporting ideas.

6. Organize ideas.

7. Formulate introduction and conclusion.

8. Prepare notes for delivery.

9. Practice.

10. Anticipate types of questions and questioners you may encounter and plan how you will respond to them.

Make an Opening Statement

How you begin is important. Your introduction will add to your listeners' initial impression of you.

You should attempt to do at least two things in your beginning remarks:

1. Try to capture your listeners' attention. Using a strong opening will catch their immediate interest.

2. Give at least a general indication of the topic and the direction of your talk. Make sure that your opening statement is related to the subject, understandable, and believable.

Try to avoid such common openings for speeches as:

- "Today I'm going to talk about. . . ."

- A joke

    —Humor is difficult for most people to use. The material has to be good and the speaker has to possess a good sense of timing. Most people fall flat on their faces with jokes.

    —Unless the joke relates to the topic of your speech, it does nothing to orient your listeners to your topic.

    —Humor can be used effectively, but be careful!

Some effective ways to begin a presentation are:

- Use a striking or memorable quotation.

- Ask a question. (You do not expect your listeners to give you a verbal response; you want them to answer to themselves.)

- Make a startling statement.

- Use a vivid illustration (verbal).

- Create suspense.

- Use a humorous story—if it relates to the topic of your speech.

Relate to Your Listeners Personally

After you have caught your listeners' attention with your opening statement, you must maintain that interest by demonstrating immediately how the subject affects them personally. Answer the question, "Why do I need to hear what you are telling me?"

Give Examples

Even after you have attracted their attention and aroused their personal interest in your idea, you still need to win over your listeners. They will most certainly want to be shown. The burden for proof is on you.

You must back up your statements with facts, proof, evidence, concrete examples, quotes. Case histories or proven systems make for good listening or reading. Also use visual material. The bulk of your perceptions come through the sense of sight. Facts are invaluable tools in maintaining interest and overcoming skepticism. Make sure any facts and figures you give are correct.

Conclude

If the speech has been a lengthy one, it is a good idea to briefly restate the major points. This will help your listeners remember what you have said.

Finally, sound a strong call to action. Your major points have been presented for some particular reason. In any presentation, the conclusion must be strong and forceful; it must be planned to answer satisfactorily the audience's legitimate question, "So what?"

To maximize the final impact, you might try one of the following methods:

- Use a striking or memorable quotation.

- Ask a question. (You expect your listeners to respond to themselves and you know what the response will be.)

- Make a startling statement.

- Give a vivid illustration.

- Tell a humorous story—if it relates.

- Issue a challenge or an appeal. (This is more useful for a persuasive speech than an informative one.)

WRITING POLICIES AND PROCEDURES

A *policy* is a statement of an objective. To write the policy:

- State your purpose.

- Determine the results you want the policy to achieve.

- Identify to whom the policy applies.

- Establish the standards for the policy. (Remember, standards should be measurable in terms of quality, quantity, or time.)

A *procedure* is a statement of how the policy is carried out. To write the procedure:

- State the purpose.

- List the necessary conditions (equipment, skills, etc.).

- Define any terms you will be using.

- Divide the process into short, simple steps.

- Label all steps with numbers (1, 2, 3) or with words indicating sequence (such as "first," "second," "next," or "then").

- Use action verbs.

- Use the imperative voice, present tense (the implied subject is always "you"). For example:

> "Engage the locking mechanism."

- Use decision tables ("if/then" tables) if the user must make a decision. For example:

If:	*Then:*
The indicator light is green	press the toggle switch
The indicator light is yellow	release the brake
The indicator light is red	remove jam from feeder belt
The light is not on	check plug in wall socket

- If a step or steps must be repeated:

  —Indicate clearly which steps must be repeated.

  —Indicate clearly when to stop the repetition (what conditions must be met before stopping). For example:

  "Repeat steps 1 through 4 until all documents have been stamped."

- If two operations must be performed simultaneously, make that clear.

  "While holding the Control key, press the F4 key."

- For complex processes, use a flow chart.

The following are samples from the "before" and "after" versions of NASA's safety handbook. The original manual was written in "legalese," was poorly organized, and mixed administrative and technical material. The new handbook has been streamlined and written in a user-friendly question and answer format. Each chapter begins with "Who must follow this chapter?" so employees no longer have to wade through irrelevant introductory material to find the information they need.

Sample Procedure
Before

Cryogenic Materials
Chapter 204
204.1 Purpose

The purpose of this chapter is to provide minimum safety requirements for the safe handling and use of the more commonly used cryogenic substances and to identify specific precautions, emergency treatment (Attachment 204A, Appendix B), protective clothing and equipment guidelines, training requirements, and housekeeping information.

Requirements set forth in this chapter shall apply to all JSC personnel performing operations that require the use, handling, or storage of cryogenic materials. Liquid oxygen or liquid hydrogen used as propellants shall follow the requirements of chapter 206, "Explosives and Propellants."

Each supervisor involved with cryogenic substances shall thoroughly understand the hazards involved, the safe handling methods, work procedures, and emergency procedures, and ensure that these procedures are understood and strictly adhered to.

Facility managers shall be familiar with the cryogenic safety and emergency procedures to ensure that they are implemented in the workplace.

Each employee working with cryogenic substances shall thoroughly understand the hazards involved, safe handling methods, work procedures, and emergency procedures.

After

This could be you . . .

Two technicians passed out while transferring liquid nitrogen from a truck because nitrogen spilled into the loading dock and displaced oxygen in the area. They were rescued and are okay. A liquid helium dewar ruptured. Fortunately, no one was in the room at the time. A liquid nitrogen dewar exploded and sent glass fragments flying. Fortunately, the technicians working with the dewar were not in the path of the flying glass.

You must follow this chapter if you:

a. Handle, store, or transfer cryogenic liquids as a part of your job.

b. Handle or work around gaseous nitrogen, oxygen, or hydrogen.

c. Supervise anyone who does the above tasks.

DRAFTING REGULATIONS

As noted earlier, government agencies at all levels—federal, state, and local—are working to word regulations in plain language. The Office of the Federal Register, National Archives and Records Administration, provides a guide to legal writing at www.nara.gov/fedreg/dldhome.html.

The topics they cover include:

• Arrangement

• Headings

- Purpose clause

- Definitions

- Ambiguity

- Principles of clear writing

- Cross-references

- Punctuation, capitalization, typography, and spelling

- Format requirements for regulatory documents

- Words and expressions to avoid

- Preferred expressions.

To show how plain language can improve legal writing, Joseph Kimble gives the following example of a before-and after provision:

Example #1: Consultant Contract

Before

The CONSULTANT agrees to fully complete the described assignment and furnish same to the DEPARTMENT by _____ calendar days after notification of Approval, it being fully understood and agreed by the parties hereto that in the event the CONSULTANT shall fail to do so as aforesaid, the DEPARTMENT shall, without the necessity of notice, terminate the services of said CONSULTANT without incurring any liability for payment for services submitted after said due date or shall deduct, as a liquidation of damages, a sum of money equal to one-third of one percent (1/3 of 1%) per calendar day of the total fee if the performance of the entire contract is delayed beyond the due date. Upon written request by the CONSULTANT an extension of time may be granted by the DEPARTMENT in writing, in the event the CONSULTANT has not received from the DEPARTMENT proper information needed to complete the assignment or, in the event other extenuating circumstances occur, the time may be similarly extended. It is further agreed that if a liquidation of damages is imposed pursuant to the aforesaid provisions, any money due and payable to the DEPARTMENT thereby may be retained out of any money earned by the CONSULTANT under the terms of this contract.

After

The Due Date for the Work

The Consultant must complete and deliver the work by _____ calendar days after receiving notice that the Department has approved this contract. The Consultant may ask in writing for more time, and the Department may grant it in writing, if

(a) the Consultant does not receive from the Department the information needed to complete the work; or

(b) there are other extenuating circumstances.

If the Consultant Misses the Due Date

If the Consultant fails to deliver the work by the due date, the Department may—without having to give notice—choose either one of the following:

(a) terminate the Consultant's services, and not pay for services that are submitted after the due date; or

(b) claim liquidated damages of 1/3 of 1% of the total contract payment for each calendar day late, and subtract this amount from the total payment.[3]

Jim Harte and Umeki Thorne, both program analysts at GSA, clarified and streamlined a 194-word rule on government-sponsored travel down to 45 words.

Example #2: Federal Travel Regulation

Before

Section 301-2.5(b) Indirect-route or interrupted travel.

When a person for his/her own convenience travels by an indirect route or interrupts travel by a direct route, the extra expenses shall be borne by him/her. Reimbursement for expenses shall be based only on such charges as would have been incurred by a usually traveled route. An employee may not use contract airline/rail passenger service provided under contract with the General Services Administration (see part 301-15, subpart B, of this chapter) for that portion of travel by an indirect route which is for personal convenience. Additionally, an employee may not use a U.S. Government Transportation Request (GTR) (see section 301-10.2 of this chapter) or a contractor-issued charge card (see part 301-15, subpart C, of this chapter) for procurement of commercial carrier transportation services for that portion of travel by an indirect route which is for personal convenience. An employee may, however, use contract airline/rail passenger service, as well as a GTR or contractor-issued charge card, for portions of travel that are authorized to be performed at

Government expense. (See section 301-11.5(a) of this chapter regarding reimbursement claims for travel that involves an indirect route.)

After

Section 301.10.8 What is my liability if, for personal convenience, I travel or use an indirect route?

If you travel on government business by anything other than the most direct, least cost route available, you must pay for the added costs so the taxpayers don't.

Because of changes in the methods and variety of workplace writing, writers, editors, and reviewers need both flexibility and team-building skills. Collaborative team writing occurs whenever two or more people are involved in writing or approving a document. Teams are more productive when they communicate clearly, coordinate their work, and understand the stages of any group.

Clear communication is also essential in the ghostwriting process. Understanding the realities of ghostwriting can help you and your partner complete the project successfully.

The budget justification describes intended outcomes that are within the agency's jurisdiction, program authority, and power. The primary purpose of a written budget is to provide friendly legislators the ammunition they need to argue your case and to justify their votes to their constituency. Effective justification statements are meaningful, measurable, clear, realistic, and comprehensive.

Whether you give a briefing to a group of four or a presentation to a packed auditorium, thorough preparation and planning are essential. Effective beginnings and conclusions especially require careful thought.

Writing policies and procedures requires absolute clarity and logical organization. A policy is a statement of an objective, while a procedure is a statement of how the policy is carried out.

Regulations and other types of legal writing benefit from the application of plain language. The Plain Language Action Network provides specific guidance for writing regulations as well as for other types of government documents.

---

[1]Piotrowski, Maryann V. *Effective Business Writing: A Guide for Those Who Write on the Job.* New York: HarperCollins, 1996, pp. 61-62.

[2]Blackerby, Phillip and Melissa Hield. "Tips on Writing Effective Budget Justifications." *Armed Forces Comptroller,* spring 1988. Used with permission.

[3]Kimble, Joseph. "Answering the Critics of Plain Language." *The Scribes Journal of Legal Writing (1994-1995).* <plainlanguage.gov/library/kimble.htm>

Answers to Exercises

CHAPTER 2

Test Yourself: Selecting the Purpose and Sequence

Read the following paragraphs. Select the paragraph that states the purpose. Put a "1" next to it. Then use the numbers 2, 3, 4, and 5 to indicate the appropriate sequence for the remaining paragraphs of the letter.

1. We are delighted that you will be speaking at our annual conference in Miami next month. I wanted to let you know as soon as possible about the arrangements for your trip.

2. We feel that you know more about the flights you wish to use than we do, so we will leave reservations in your hands. As you know, we will reimburse you for tourist class travel, round trip between your home and Miami, and for ground transportation in your own city. You can submit the airfare and ground costs with the billing for your professional fee.

3. When you arrive at the airport, Terry Mills will get in touch with you. Terry is our on-site conference coordinator and will personally escort you to the Hospitality Hotel for check-in.

4. All the food expenses in Miami will be taken care of for you. Luncheons are buffets in the ballroom—you can just go in and help yourself. When you register at the

hotel you will receive tickets for dinner on the day of your presentation. Just sign your breakfast bills so we can pay them with your hotel bill.

5. Please phone me collect if you have any unanswered questions, or if we have forgotten some detail. You can reach me at (505) 444-8881, extension 11.

Question: What type of organization did you use?

Answer: Chronological.

CHAPTER 3

Test Yourself: Organizing Paragraphs

A. Putting the Main Idea Up Front; Cutting Ideas that Don't Belong

Read over the seven sentences that follow. Then decide how you would make a unified, well-planned paragraph out of them.

Perhaps the most important thing to be said about conversation is that practice is essential to improvement and that you can practice on your own without waiting for an audience to come along. One way to practice is selecting a subject in your spare moments and making yourself say something about it as quickly as possible. The subjects may come from newspaper headlines, magazine contents, book or chapter titles, and overheard remarks. Once you have decided on a subject, you can discipline yourself to pull your thoughts together and commence your own statement on the subject within seconds. Sometimes you will continue to talk spontaneously on the subject until you run out of material; at other times you may set a goal of talking for two or three minutes.

B. Making New Paragraphs

Expressed in a single paragraph, the material that follows looks massive and uninviting. How would you break it up into four paragraphs? Indicate where you would make the paragraph breaks by inserting paragraph symbols (¶).

A process is any series of actions in a sequence that brings about a particular result or condition. Studying is a process. So is driving a car, getting dressed, doing research, manufacturing something, or performing a laboratory experiment. Processes include not only fairly simple procedures, methods, techniques, and activities, but also complex ones.

A process can be described as a series of continuous actions from (1) the point of view of an observer or onlooker, or (2) the point of view of the participant or doer of the actions. If the purpose is merely to inform the reader, the process is described from the point of view of the observer. If the purpose is to give instructions to someone who is to perform the process, the description of the process should be written from the point of view of a participant. The two viewpoints, however, should never be mixed in describing a particular process. To mix the two would confuse the reader completely.

Regardless of which viewpoint is used, it often is necessary to include illustrations. Such illustrations may include photographs, drawings, flow charts, graphs, tables, diagrams, or schematics as needed to show individual actions in sequence.

When describing and explaining a process it is usually desirable to follow a fairly well standardized pattern—one that has become standardized not because of arbitrary considerations but because it leads to explanations that are easy to understand. This pattern calls for an introduction, an overall picture including a list of the main steps that make up the process, an explanation of each step listed, and a conclusion if it seems that one would be helpful.

Test Yourself: Writing Topic Sentences

In the space at the top of each of the following paragraphs, add a topic sentence:

The following are some examples:

1. A well-written sentence has several elements.

2. Candidates for the position should have at least four years of experience, a college degree, and skill in interpersonal relations.

Test Yourself: Overloaded Sentences

"The statements were made by Richard N. Wilson, Project Director for the Southern Regional Center, a federally funded, department-sponsored project. The Center does research for participating agencies in Region IV, which includes Kentucky, Tennessee, North Carolina, South Carolina, Georgia, Alabama, Mississippi, and Florida."

Test Yourself: Sound Sentences

A. Some of the following sentences are complete. Others are run-on sentences, while others are sentence fragments. In front of the number for each sentence, put the symbol that applies:

    C for complete sentence
    R for run-on sentence
    F for sentence fragment

1. F	6. C
2. R	7. C
3. C	8. R
4. C	9. C
5. F	10. F

B. *Make complete sentences out of these fragments:*

1. While we are on the subject, don't forget to call Gen. Johnston.

2. Please take these over to the files.

3. Feeling lost, the new employee in my office went to the boss for help.

C. *Insert or substitute proper punctuation to remedy these run-on sentences.*

1. You don't have to be concerned about it. I'll take care of it.

2. On the one hand, we can take the positive view and hope the problem solves itself; on the other hand, we can take action to solve it immediately.

3. There are two methods of sampling: They are the simple random sample method (which assigns each individual name a number and then draws numbers) and the area sampling method (which selects city blocks of individuals).

Test Yourself: Rewriting Tom's Letter

Re-read the case study at the beginning of this chapter. Take the suggestions given by Bob and rewrite Tom's paragraph.

Honesty is the hallmark of Marcia's character. Her honesty extends from areas where we easily see it (in relationships and business transactions) to integrity of thought. Scientific, thorough, and meticulous, she approaches any analytical task with an exacting eye. This is what I mean by integrity of thought.

I have always been impressed by Marcia's helpfulness and willingness to help others, regardless of their position. She also is pleasant to work with, and she takes the time to help those who are learning their way. For example, last week, she stayed late to help a co-worker complete a task that was behind schedule.

CHAPTER 4

Test Yourself: Giving Sentences Action by Changing Passive to Active Voice

The following are suggested answers.

1. Thank you for your patience.

2. Each chapter includes exercises.

3. We hope you will resolve this matter promptly.

4. This section requires a new machine.

5. This chart summarizes our recommendations.

6. My boss transferred the assignment to me last week.

7. We are trying to bite off more than we can chew.

8. When the alarm sounds, shut down the machine at once.

9. All department heads have completed this survey.

10. We have negotiated with the contractor several times.

11. We have concluded that the process should not be changed.

12. Hiring a temporary worker requires signing a contract with an agency.

Test Yourself: Bringing Submerged Verbs to the Surface

The following are suggested answers.

1. These charts depict the results of our survey.

2. We recommend investigating these findings.

3. Management example strongly influences employee behavior.

4. These reports explain our findings.

5. My boss transferred responsibility to me last week.

6. We believe these changes would be too costly.

7. When the red light indicates overheating, shut the machine off.

8. The report has been analyzed. (*NOTE: This is an exception to the rule against using passive voice; however, if the writer knew who analyzed the report, it would be better to say so—"Bob analyzed the report," for example.*)

9. We have evaluated your proposal thoroughly.

10. After carefully reviewing the evidence, we decided that pursuing the matter further is not justified.

11. Temporarily reassigning an employee requires a transfer arrangement.

12. We confirmed the contract yesterday.

Test Yourself: Say It in a Friendlier Way

The following are suggested answers.

1. We forwarded your letter to the Personnel Department. (*The accusatory tone of "you wrote to the wrong department" has been removed.*)

2. You may call me during business hours if you have any questions. (*The statement, "If the points I've made aren't clear to you," which suggests the reader might be too stupid to understand, has been removed.*)

3. Please sign the application so that we can proceed.

4. We will be happy to process your order when you make payment arrangements. (*Note that the accusatory tone of "failed to enclose" has been removed.*)

5. We have not received your June 30 report. (*Note that the accusatory "allegedly" has been removed, and that the month in question has been specified to avoid confusion.*)

6. Please let us know as soon as possible your decision on using the space. (*Note that the demanding tone of "We need to hear from you" has been replaced by a more respectful request.*)

7. These are the steps you should take in filing a claim. (*Note the friendlier, less impersonal tone.*)

8. We are handling your request as quickly as possible. (*Note the use of the friendlier "We" instead of the impersonal passive voice.*)

9. Your cooperation will help make this program a success. (*Note that this version makes a friendly call for cooperation, instead of making it a requirement.*)

10. Filling out the form will ensure that the survey reflects your opinion. (*Note that this version eliminates the "or else" implied in the original.*)

11. Please return this report after review. (*Note the more friendly, less impersonal tone.*)

12. Please sign and date the enclosed form if you want this change.

CHAPTER 5

Test Yourself: Finding a Better Way to Say It

Suggested answers

1. We agree to your request.

2. Enclosed is a check for $19.95.

3. Our plan has several merits.

4. The appendix is being sent separately.

5. This is confidential.

6. I apologize if this is tardy and causes any inconvenience.

7. Please respond by _____.

8. We have not received the proposal.

Test Yourself: Deflating Words

Suggested answers

1. work

2. end

3. meet

4. broken

5. set priorities

6. since

7. use

8. who

9. best

10. aware

Test Yourself: Deflating Sentences

Suggested answers

1. You will move ahead faster and make more money as you make the best use of your abilities.

2. We believe your plan for reducing injuries will not work.

3. The current procedure does not make the best use of our personnel.

4. Radioactivity is currently a possibility. (*When is radioactivity* not *excessively dangerous? Note also that "presently" can mean either "right now" or "soon." Use another, more specific word.*)

5. Most students were not well prepared, and they made many mistakes.

Test Yourself: Making the Parts Parallel

Suggested answers

A.

1. Planning and Preparing

    a. Setting objectives

    b. Determining what is negotiable

    c. Recognizing vulnerabilities

2. Formulating an Opening Position

3. Making an Effective Presentation

    a. Making a good first impression

    b. Opening a channel of communications

4. Reaching Agreement

5. Implementing an Agreement

B.

- Making higher earnings over one's working life

- Relating current events to the past

- Acquiring specialized knowledge

- Becoming familiar with the cultural side of life

- Gaining insight into the human experience

C.

1. The report discussing problem solving accompanies the one discussing decision making.

2. The team spent a week in the field and visited several offices.

3. Their staff members are friendly and efficient.

D.

Introduction

Study Methodology

Major Problems

Other Problems

Recommendations

Conclusion

E. Answers will vary.

Test Yourself: Painting a Clear Picture

Read the following statements.

Now read into them. Use your imagination.

Replace each statement with one that is specific. Make it interesting and informative. Write more than one sentence if you like.

1. The study related to energy.

   The National Science Foundation's study, published this month, compares the costs of supplying energy from four different sources over the past two decades.

2. The meeting was well attended.

   Records show that 565 people attended the Technology Convention in 2001, up 35% from the previous year.

3. I work hard.

   I work approximately 50 hours a week in the office and an additional 10-12 hours each weekend at home.

4. Their time-management problem needs attention.

   John and Martha both have been arriving 15-30 minutes late each day. They need to get to work on time.

5. The idea got a good reception.

   Ninety-eight percent of the employees voted in favor of a flexible work policy.

6. They are uptight about the project.

    They are so uptight about the customer service project that they refused to answer any of my questions and would not join us for the employee lunch.

CHAPTER 7

Test Yourself: Line Editing a Letter

Suppose the letter below were going out over your signature. What changes would you make before it is mailed? Examine the letter for things that look or sound strange. Look out for inconsistencies, omissions, errors, problems with tone and style, submerged verbs, and parts that are not parallel. Is the letter understandable? Is the phrasing precise? Circle each mistake you notice and rewrite the letter.

Dear Mrs. Jones:

The following is a summary of changes planned for this year's Youth Leadership Institute (YLI) program.

Screening of Instructors

More than 70% of our participants said that last year's YLI program was the best leadership-training program in the state. However, the program showed the need to provide 24-hour monitoring of program participants. Therefore, the Behavioral Sciences Department suggested that this year's instructors undergo new screening procedures. This screening would identify whether instructors have:

- background in psychology needed for providing 24-hour monitoring of students;

- crisis counseling abilities; and

- any substance abuse problems.

We are preparing to begin the screening this year, with help from the Behavioral Sciences and Personnel departments.

Improved Survey

We have found that we need a better way to measure our participants' progress during the program. Each year we ask students to evaluate their progress at the YLI program. Unfortunately, students last year seemed unwilling to discuss their concerns, so the evaluation did not reflect students' progress accurately.

Therefore, we are developing a new survey that uses both instructor-led interviews and anonymous questionnaires. Both surveys will be administered biweekly. Students will participate in both programs, and instructors will use the anonymous questionnaire results to gauge the overall progress of the students. We hope to have more accurate results with this new system.

Thank you for your interest in the YLI program. We will send you copies of all pertinent forms and questionnaires when they become available. Please call if you need more information.

Sincerely,

CHAPTER 8

Test Yourself: Stating the Subject and Purpose

Give each email a more informative subject statement. Then write a one-sentence or two-sentence opening that makes the purpose clear. The following are examples.

SUBJECT: Equal Opportunity Employment Directive

Attached are this company's equal employment opportunity policy and a copy of the Equal Employment Opportunity Law. This directive makes equal employment opportunity official policy in our company.

SUBJECT: Action Items from Oct. 24 Meeting

Please review the following and let me know if there are any omissions or inaccuracies.

Test Yourself: Writing a Short Email

Write the subject statement and the body of a brief email to the division chief.

The following is a suggested answer.

SUBJECT: Delay of Cotton Comfortwear Inspection

I found out this morning that Cotton Comfortwear operators have filed papers in court to keep us off their property. Because of this court action, I told our inspection team today to stay off the mill property. The inspection scheduled for Aug. 4, 5, and 6 is on hold until I receive further information from you and from the legal branch.

Please advise.

CHAPTER 9

Test Yourself: Writing a Letter Using Headings

VETERANS BENEFITS ADMINISTRATION
Pension Medical Evidence

Addressee
Street
City
State/zip

Dear addressee:

We have your claim for a pension. Our laws require us to ask you for more information. The information you give us will help us decide whether we can pay you a pension.

What We Need

Send us a medical report from a doctor or clinic that you visited in the past six months. The report should show why you can't work.

Please take this letter and the enclosed doctor's guide to your doctor.

When We Need It

We need the doctor's report by [date]. We'll have to turn down your claim if we don't get the report by that date.

Your Right to Privacy

The information you give us is private. We might have to give out this information in a few special cases. But we will not give it out to the general public without your permission. We've attached a form that explains your privacy rights. If you have any questions, call us toll-free by dialing 1-800-827-1000. Our tdd number for the hearing-impaired is 1-800-829-4833. If you call, please have this letter with you.

Sincerely,

Test Yourself: Creating an If-Then Table

§ 163.17 What deposit must I make with my bid?
You must include with your proposal to buy Indian forest products a deposit that meets the conditions in the following table.

If the appraised stumpage value is . . .	you must deposit . . .	and the minimum amount of the deposit is . . .
less than $100,000	ten percent of the stumpage value	$1,000 or full value, whichever is less
between $100,000 and $250,000	five percent of the stumpage value	$10,000
over $250,000	three percent of the stumpage value	$12,500

CHAPTER 10

Test Yourself: The Report's Tone

Bennett County Hospital
Preliminary Report 2
June 16, 2000

Submitted to
The Board of Trustees
by
The Review Committee

We are pleased to submit the second of three reports that you requested for your study of the feasibility of expanding Bennett County Hospital. We will submit the third report within three months and will include the data that you requested in your December 2, 1999, letter.

General Information

For the first time, the Bennett County Hospital has received full accreditation from the highest national authority on hospital accreditation, the Joint Commission on Accreditation of Hospitals.

The hospital received this full accreditation because its personnel, services, and physical plant meet or exceed high professional standards.

In the past year, the hospital took the following steps to enhance the quality of service provided:

- Upgraded intensive care facilities

- Made a comparative study of nurses' salaries

- Increased nurses' salaries in order to maintain a well-qualified staff

- Began holding monthly meetings to maintain the cooperation of staff, administration, and trustees....

CHAPTER 11

Test Yourself: Writing a Mechanism Description

For a computer, a mouse is a device used to select commands, text, or screen objects. A mouse can only be used on computers with a graphical interface computer system, such as Windows. Such computers allow the user to communicate with the computer using graphic symbols instead of keyboard strokes. Commonly, users operate a mouse frequently throughout an entire work session.

A mouse is designed to fit into an adult's hand. It has one or more buttons on top, usually located at the end of the mouse furthest away from the user's palm. This placement allows the user to press the button(s) with one finger (a process known as "clicking"). A mouse also has a small ball on the underside. The ball floats freely within the mouse case and can rotate in any direction. The mouse sits on a flat surface and is connected to the computer's hard drive by a thin cable (resembling a mouse's tail).

To operate the mouse, the user rests his or her hand lightly atop it and slides it gently across the flat surface. Doing so causes the ball underneath to move. As the ball moves, a symbol moves on the screen. The symbol, known as a mouse pointer, shows the active position of the mouse (the element on the screen that will be affected if the user clicks on the mouse button). By pointing the mouse and clicking the buttons, the user selects the desired command, text, or object on the screen.[1]

_____

[1]*Technical Writing Skills*, Vienna, VA: Management Concepts, Inc., 1996.

Index